PENGUIN BOOKS

THE MAN IN THE RUBBER MASK

Robert Llewellyn was born in 1956 and educated in various Midland schools before becoming a professional hippie craftsman. He graduated through rune-decorated leather work to orthopaedic shoes, living in a variety of squats and furniture lorries until he stepped on to a stage at twenty-five.

He has been writing all his life. His first novel, *The Case of the Brocen Lok*, amounting to a full twenty-five pages, was completed when he was nine. His stage work provided an outlet and he wrote sketches, plays and Channel 4 sitcoms throughout the 1980s, culminating in the prize-winning *Mammon, Robot Born of Woman* in 1988. He has appeared in *Red Dwarf* since 1989. *The Reconstructed Heart*, his first book, was published in 1992.

ROBERT
LLEWELLYN

The Man in the
Rubber Mask

PENGUIN BOOKS

PENGUIN BOOKS

Published by the Penguin Group
Penguin Books Ltd, 27 Wrights Lane, London w8 5tz, England
Penguin Books USA Inc., 375 Hudson Street, New York, New York 10014, USA
Penguin Books Australia Ltd, Ringwood, Victoria, Australia
Penguin Books Canada Ltd, 10 Alcorn Avenue, Toronto, Ontario, Canada m4v 3b2
Penguin Books (NZ) Ltd, 182–190 Wairau Road, Auckland 10, New Zealand

Penguin Books Ltd, Registered Offices: Harmondsworth, Middlesex, England

First published 1994
10 9 8 7 6 5 4 3 2

Set by Datix International Limited, Bungay, Suffolk
Filmset in 11/14 pt Monophoto Bembo
Printed in England by Clays Ltd, St Ives plc

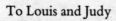
To Louis and Judy

CHAPTER 1

In the giant control room in the sky, there are banks and banks of lights on a huge, smooth, black control board, each one connected to an emotion, or a significant experience, of a human being on earth. If only we were aware of them, our lives would be transformed. If only I knew that my irony warning light had been burning so regularly over the last five years they kept having to replace the bulb. The irony light was full on, I now see, when I was carrying the last bag of props down seven flights of stone steps in that Edinburgh apartment building. It was on because I thought carrying seven bags of props was hard work. The rest of the world was sitting around chatting and having tea, having sex, or sleeping off the copious poisons of a night's debauchery. How come, I thought, I was heaving great big boxes of heavy stuff about so early on a Sunday morning?

It was the beginning of September in 1988, the end of the Edinburgh International Festival of theatre, music, dance, poetry, opera, jazz, film, television and shagging. I always had the feeling that there was a lot of the latter going on in Edinburgh, in between all the former.

It was the time of year when Edinburgh turns into a thespian village. This was a concept which came from some old luvvie★ who made an opening speech at the Festival club along the lines of, 'Once a year the City of Edinburgh is turned into a giant thespian village.'

Apart from shagging and thespians, there was an astonishing amount of drinking taking place, astonishing for me because I don't drink very much. Half a pint of watered-down lager and I'm performing a sad strip-a-gram on a bar-room table before you can say, Keep your dignity. If I drink a double whisky I'm transformed into a smiling human vomit cannon in about thirty seconds, so I stick to orange juice and very expensive mineral water.

However, unlike most non-drinkers, I quite enjoy the company of drunk people.† There are two bars at the Edinburgh Festival where people I know lean against the wall and talk a lot. The Assembly Rooms and the Gilded Balloon. In the Assembly Rooms, we all stand around under huge, posh chandeliers, shouting and laughing in a loud show-off sort of way. All the time we are talking to someone, we are looking around the room hoping to meet someone really famous. It's a complaint called Edinburgh neck, an involuntary spinal twitch which ruins any

---

★ Grand old Actor.

† There have been some notable exceptions to this rule. A noisy drunken party which started at four-thirty in the morning made me a bit depressed once. Depressed being a polite, middle-class way of saying deeply angry.

conversation and reduces all communication to gag try-out and witty put-down. The room is packed full of insecure, loud-mouthed performers, agents and TV executives. I love it.

The Gilded Balloon bar is slightly different. It is where the exact same crowd go when they are pretending they hate the Assembly Rooms bar. I love doing that. I love going to the Gilded Balloon after I have been in the Assembly Rooms, twitching my head like a demented automaton, and then slagging everyone off for being so posy. 'I can't stand the Assembly Rooms. It's just utterly full of people looking around to see who's in. I mean, Lenny* and Dawn† walked in, and everyone looked at them. It's pathetic.'

I said this to Arthur Smith, the man who played the barman in *Backwards*,‡ and he said to me, 'I met Lenny Henry once, well, I didn't actually meet him, I saw him at a party.'

The Gilded Balloon bar isn't quite as glamorous as the Assembly Rooms. It is, in fact, a narrow corridor leading to the toilet, but it will accommodate up to one hundred and seventy very drunk comedians. Drunk comedians stand very close to you when they are in full flow. They tell you what you should do with your show, your life and your lover. By three in the morning, it can begin to look rather sad,

* Henry.
† French.
‡ *Red Dwarf III.*

3

and if you are not deeply relaxed after seven pints of designer lager then the best bet is to head for home.

The final bag was stuffed into my small, rusty hatchback car, and we set off. I breathed in the crisp Scottish air and brewery fumes for the last time, little knowing that by the time I got twelve miles down the road, one of the new super-cheap remould tyres I had bought to get the car through its MOT would tear apart like a wet paper bag in a wind tunnel.

My two companions, Martin Pople (who could have gone out with Greta Scaatchi, but didn't) and Deborah John Wilson (whose brother is Yafek Koto, the black guy in the original *Alien* movie) sat on the side of the road laughing as I struggled to get the spare wheel out from under the monstrous amount of stuff we were carrying. By some fluke the spare wheel was pumped up, I found a jack and a spanner, so after a few more comedy wheel-changing moments we were on our way.

The reason I had super-cheap, fell-off-the-back-of-a-lorry, good-as-new tyres on the car was because I was skint. This was my normal state of affairs, nothing to worry about, I got by, somehow, it was only odd because I had just completed a sell-out run of a play I had written called (and you should read this bit as if you were announcing an upcoming science fiction movie, the classic deep American rumble voice) *Mammon, Robot Born of Woman*.

It had been nominated for the Perrier Award.* Plays don't normally get nominated, stand-up comics normally get nominated, so that meant it must have been good, even though it didn't actually win. Not that I cared of course, I'm not competitive, I'm a thespian, I didn't care when Simon Fanshaw† gave me a big hug in the bar of the Assembly Rooms and told me with barely concealed delight that I hadn't won. 'Robbie, darling!' he shouted. 'You haven't won, isn't it absolutely dreadful!'

The play was about a robot, as you can probably tell from the title, not at all like Kryten. Mammon was supposed to be a robot who resembled a human to such a degree that no one other than his maker could tell that he wasn't. It was the Frankenstein story, mixed with a bit of *Robocop*, bit of *Terminator* and a few silly walks. The twist was that instead of the maker being a mad male scientist, she was a mad female scientist. Dawn Raid (played by Deborah John Wilson) was black and had made the perfect white man in order to enter the market place or the Stock Exchange and start making money. Remember, this was 1988, before Black Wednesday, Black

---

* An award funded by the Perrier water company. First prize is a thousand pounds, and all nominees get to do their show in London at the Donmar Warehouse.

† Big, loud, gay stand-up comic, wit, raconteur and one-time co-presenter on *That's Life* with Esther Rantzen. Now has a hand in the Brighton Comedy Festival.

Friday and that rather dull grey Tuesday morning in early April. At this time there were still wide-boys in the City of London pulling down 800K a year gross and thinking they were terribly clever. I was brought up to believe it was very bad manners to laugh at other people's misfortune, but the day after Black Wednesday I cycled through the City of London laughing my head off and pointing at sad, dejected-looking businessmen in their crumpled pinstripes. It was an amazing sight to see so many deeply unhappy seriously rich people.

In the story Mammon made money on the stock market very successfully, but as he progressed Dawn noticed he started to develop certain human characteristics. He was designed to blend in with his environment, which is what he did. He started to become like the men he worked with. Dawn, being a slightly mad scientist, took the next step: she introduced lust mode 691, the ultimate in sexuality software, into Mammon's computer brain. At this point Mammon copulated with everything on the stage, including some members of the audience unlucky enough to be seated in the front row. It was a disgusting spectacle and should have been banned.

I remember thinking, during those rare moments of speculative thought actors have during performing, that it was an odd thing for a grown man to be doing. Pretending to copulate with a desk in front of 200 people in a small room in Edinburgh. Little did I know the irony warning light was flickering on the big control panel in the sky. I had seen nothing yet.

With a new super-cheap remould tyre fitted to the super-cheap car, we continued our journey south. I dropped Deborah off in Manchester, Martin in Leicester. I drove the last leg of the journey alone, arriving in London in the early hours of the morning, dumped all the props and bags in the hall, listened to the three messages on my answer machine from my mum, and collapsed into bed.

One of the first things I did the following day was go through the press list to see who had come to see the play. During the hectic schedule of doing the show every day, I took only the barest note of what people said to me. All sorts of heavyweight (as in influential, not as in tubby) media people came to see the show, and as I scanned the list I saw a name that I knew. Paul Jackson. I knew he did *The Young Ones*, and loads of other things. He was one of those people who did a lot of stuff on telly.

About nine months later (the usual gestation period for babies and weird events) I locked my push-bike to a lamppost on the Charing Cross Road. I was going to have a meeting with the same Paul Jackson, and some other blokes, about some sort of part in some sort of sitcom. That's all I knew. I entered the little door at the offices of the Noel Gay agency and was met by Paul Jackson's braces and tie. As the glowing sensation settled in my eyeballs, I shook hands with the figure behind. Paul immediately showed me downstairs, where I entered a basement office to see three men sitting round a table: a tall gangly skinny one called Ed, and two slightly shorter stockier ones called Rob and Doug, together known as Grant Naylor. As soon as I was told their names I forgot because, as Rob, Doug and Ed would no doubt confirm, I have a memory like a sieve.

We talked about robots and funny walks and accents and especially trying to avoid all the old comedy robots like R2D2 and Marvin the Paranoid Android. Looking back, it was the first time I experienced the Grant Naylor gaze, those four eyes which record every tiny nuance of your behaviour and start to reprogram it in their weird heads so two years later you find yourself in costume doing something oddly similar.

After this meeting I realized what they were talking about. I had seen about three episodes of *Red Dwarf*.

I knew Norman Lovett, who played Holly the computer in the first two series, from the stand-up comedy circuit. He was replaced by Hattie Hayridge when I joined in the third series so I never worked with him on *Red Dwarf* but we had worked together on various things over the years, including my first-ever experience of working in television. It was on a Channel 4 show called, wait for it, this *is* what it was called, I promise you, *Book 'em and Risk It!* It had the exclamation mark at the end of it like that. *Book 'em and Risk It!* Brilliant.

I saw Norman regularly over the next eight years or so. One very memorable time was when I was compere at a comedy club in Woolwich, South London, called the Tramshed. Just before I went on stage to announce him, Norman asked me to time him from when he went on stage to when he first spoke. I nodded, not really understanding what he was asking, went on to the stage and said, 'Ladies and gentlemen, please put your hands together in a warm and supportive manner for the very wonderful Mister Norman Lovett.' The crowd went bananas and Norman sloped on to the stage looking slightly moth-eaten and miserable. He stood behind the microphone, the clapping died down, the room became quieter as the audience waited for the first gag. Norman stood there in silence. Someone laughed, Norman looked at them, the whole audience laughed. He looked at the whole audience. They laughed again. Norman hadn't uttered a sound. I was looking at my watch at the side of the stage, two minutes. The other comics on that night crowded around. They knew Norman was going for his record. He stood motionless, picked out by the single spotlight. The audience went silent again, not a sound. Norman stared at them. It was a comic's nightmare, standing there in utter silence. Then someone snickered, Norman gave the person the most cursory of glances and immediately the whole audience started laughing again. Four minutes. He'd been standing on the stage in front of three hundred people for four minutes, entertaining them, somehow, by doing absolutely nothing. It was very funny, it was utterly infectious, even the hardened old pros at the side of the stage were roaring with laughter. There must have been ten periods of nerve-racking silence, each one broken by someone bursting out laughing, looking at this gaunt, miserable bloke standing on a stage, wearing a cardigan. At seven minutes twenty seconds, after a huge prolonged wave of laughter, Norman said, 'What?' and he got a terrific ovation.

Anyway, I'd seen Norman's face in this sitcom set in space, with Craig Charles, who I'd seen in the bar of the Assembly Rooms in Edinburgh. There was another man with an H on his forehead whom I recognized. It was Chris Barrie. I'd seen him at the Comedy Store, years before, doing amazing impressions. E-e-e-e-e-e-e-extraordinary David Coleman. Then another man came in, he had amazing clothes on, and big teeth, he was called Cat. I didn't know him. I'd never seen him anywhere. That's because I hadn't been to see the three hundred West End musicals Danny John Jules had already found Divadom in.

About three weeks after that first meeting with Rob, Doug, Ed and Paul Jackson, I drove into the BBC special effects department in Acton. I didn't know what I was letting myself in for. I was, like most of the world's population, a prosthetic virgin. If only I'd been aware of the irony warning light flashing in the heavens when I'd spoken to Rob and Doug. I had explained to them that I was slightly concerned about playing a robot, or a mechanoid, because I was midway through developing a series for Channel 4 about a robot, based on my Edinburgh play, and I didn't want to get typecast. Rob and Doug assured me that it wouldn't be a problem, they thought that very few people would recognize me. I think it's important to remember that I was very reassured by this. When I say important, I mean to keep the concept of this importance in context. It wasn't very important in the grand scheme of things, like, it wouldn't be very important to someone in Northern Thailand, or in the Horn of Africa. It was only important to me, for about a minute, which isn't very high on a world rating of important things.

I entered the special effects room and was greeted by Peter Wragg, the shaman, the genius, the man behind *Thunderbirds*, the quiet, retiring master of special effects. 'This shouldn't take too long, Robert,' he said. 'We're just going to cover your head with dental mould and about fifteen pounds of plaster bandage. D'you want a cup of tea?'

He led me through rooms where men in white overalls were making exploding chairs for Noel Edmonds' *Big Big Breakfast Show*. This was the room they made the Daleks in, the Cybermen's wellington boots were sprayed silver in this very building. Everywhere I looked there were old rubber monsters, slavering beasts with eyes on stalks, severed heads and rubber arms, model spaceships and boats, men sitting at benches sawing small bits of metal.

We entered a room white with plaster dust, where I met Bethan Jones who was head of the *Red Dwarf* make-up department. She was Welsh and as soon as I walked into the room she said, 'I knew you weren't really Welsh, I knew you'd be fake Welsh.'

I took great umbrage at this. Fake Welsh, with a name like Llewellyn! Of course the truth is that I'm about as Welsh as a croissant, but somewhere in my past there must have been a couple of Taffs. Peter and Bethan Jones discussed my head, Peter pointing at the bridge of my nose with a pen. 'If we can carve in here quite steeply,' he said, 'we'll get a better shape in the forehead.'

What were they going to do? Put my head in a vice and get out a chisel? I wanted to look at the small print in my contract. I could see it clearly in my mind's eye. Why hadn't I look at this more closely?

> Section 4(a) Subsection F9
> Clause 18
> The artist shall render his head, face and all areas above the throat to the company for modification, enhancement and radical change. All surgery costs and corrective therapy needed after the production to be paid for by the artist.

I didn't remember reading that bit. As I sat in the chair which was placed in the middle of the room, I was assured by Peter Wragg that I wasn't about to have radical surgery.

'Some people,' said Bethan Jones, as she stuck a rubber bald cap over my hair, 'go completely mad when their heads are covered in plaster of Paris. D'you think you'll be all right?'

I didn't know how to answer. It was like being asked, Some people completely die when they have a steamroller drive over them. D'you think you'll survive? Having never had my head covered in plaster-of-Paris bandage, it was difficult to judge. I didn't think I was claustrophobic, I'm a pretty well-balanced sort of guy, most of the time.

As my body was wrapped in black bin bags, I began to get the distinct impression I wasn't going to have a lot of choice in the matter. I was going to get covered whether I went mad or not.

'Here's a pad of paper and a pen,' said Peter, handing me the same. 'This is in case you need something scratching when you're under. Just write down which bit is itching, we'll try and scratch it, then put a tick if we've got it. You won't be able to speak, hear, see or smell anything while you're under.' I gripped the pen and paper as if they were my last hope.

'We start with the mouth and nose,' said Peter, who was now mixing a large plastic bowl full of bright yellow stuff which looked a bit like putty. 'This is alginate, the stuff they make dental moulds out of, it's quite minty in taste, but it is a bit cold when we first put it on.' I nodded in the special way I have developed when I don't understand anything but want it to appear that I do.

'We cover your nose and mouth first, then you blow through your nose and we make a little hole for you to breathe through. We need it to actually go in your mouth, so can you keep your mouth open very slightly. OK?'

As I nodded yes, Peter slapped a great big handful of this minty gloop right in my face. It was very cold, it covered my nose, went into my mouth, forced my lips apart, ran over my teeth, settled around my tongue and went sort of rubbery hard. It was like eating minty custard that went solid as you ate it. It was like being covered in semi-solid tooth-paste, it was like nothing else I had ever experienced. They covered my eyes next, then my neck, ears, top of my head. Their voices became muffled, all the sound was distorted as I felt something heavy and wet being slopped on top of the minty rubbery goo. I assumed this would be the plaster-of-Paris bandage. I felt a lot of rubbing and squibbling about, and my head started to get heavier. All I could hear was my breathing, all of which was taking place through one nostril, which naturally, after a few minutes, started to itch. And I mean itch, like the itch at the centre of the universe. What could I do? It must only have been seconds, but it seemed like ages. My whole consciousness was focused on this itchy nostril. I tried to wipe it from my brain, I tried to think about sex, car crashes, mountain streams in the dappled sunlight. Wide-open seascapes, the mountains outside Vancouver. Anything except this damn nostril. Then I remembered the pen and paper I was holding in my sweaty little hands. I wrote, as best I could without seeing the paper, NOSTRILITCH. I heard muffled voices and movement around me, but I couldn't tell what was going on, until I suddenly felt something poke up my nostril. I found out later it was one of those blue make-up-removal things with cotton wool spun on each end. It did the trick, the relief was monumental. In the normal course of events, an itchy nostril is hardly something you comment on. You don't call a halt to a conversation and say, Hold it! Wait! I've got an itchy nostril, everyone stay calm. You just rub it, pick it and flick it, and be done with it. Not so when your head is encased in seven pounds of plaster of Paris.

My steady, regular breathing continued, in, out, in, out. I became super aware that I was an animal, that I had lungs which were two big bags which had to fill with air, then blow it out again. Then I could hear my pulse, thrubub, thrubub. I could almost see my heart, this funny pumpy thing which keeps going, day and night, until I pop my clogs. How does it know? Why doesn't it just forget to beat, why don't I just snuff it? I felt my heart rate increase, thrub thrub thrub, I felt a small rush of adrenaline, maybe I would die with this bloody thing on my head. Maybe they wouldn't be able to get it off and I would starve to death slowly. I'd never see anyone again, my girlfriend, my mates, my mum and dad. It was all over. I could see the headlines, PRINCESS DI HAS LADDER IN TIGHTS SHOCK. Let's face it, who would write about some sad actor who starved to death inside a plaster-of-Paris head mould in the BBC special effects department in Acton?

I tried to control these maddening day-dreams, I tried to think about sex. Great big heaving . . . pulsating sweating . . . it didn't work. It was a big shock. Never before in my life had I been unable to have a kinky sexual fantasy. I'd had them during exams at school, I'd had them when I was failing my driving test, I'd had them when I was having sex! But now, in this little, quiet private world, where no one would know, because even if the Bishop raised his hat, I was totally covered in loose-fitting black plastic, it wasn't working. It didn't matter, I just could not think about nobbing, I couldn't even manage a soft-core hair shampoo advert. It was the ideal opportunity to have some deeply kinky and perverted sexual thoughts. Not a sausage. In fact, a sausage would have been about the kinkiest thing I could have thought about. What a breakthrough though, for sex offenders. They get sentenced to ten hours a day with their head cased in plaster of Paris. It just stops all that stuff. Well, it did for me. Maybe it wouldn't work for everyone. I bet there's some bloke somewhere who is rock hard for plaster of Paris. I bet there's a magazine you can buy in an Amsterdam bookshop called, *Kinky Plaster of Paris Monthly*. Well, it's not so daft, I've seen a magazine called *Enema Digest*. When I was doing legitimate research of course. Actually, I don't want to go on about plaster of Paris for ever, but I have to point out there were also the Chicago Plaster Casters. This was a team of young women artists in the late sixties who went around making plaster casts of famous rock stars' . . . well, what can I call it and not be juvenile, let me think. Stiffies, yes, that's mature. First, they made them go . . . like they do, and then they covered them with plaster of Paris. Once it had set they filled them with wax and a bit of string and made candles out of them.

Oh, all right, I admit, I tried it. I saw this document-ary about mad American sex therapists which had a section about these women. I was young, I was impressionable, I went home and tried it. I had a bit of plaster of Paris left over from building hills for my model railway set. I was halfway through the process, I don't want to go into details but it seemed to be working, when suddenly my mother called to me from downstairs that it was teatime. I quickly tried to remove two and a half pounds of semi-hard plaster from my semi-hard manhood. I had forgotten one vital element. The Chicago Plaster Casters used a plastic sheet with a hole in it to avoid the plaster of Paris getting caught on the model's pubic hair. OK, OK, it's gross, I know, but anyway, I didn't know that.

There is no real way of describing the pain that comes from hanging two-and-a-half pounds of plaster of Paris from three or four pubic hairs, but let's just agree that it is intense. I was panicking, I knew my mum was going to walk into my bedroom and I was going to suffer some fairly hefty adolescent humili-ation. Luckily, I had a pair of nail-scissors on my bedside table and with a bit of judicious snipping I managed to remove the offending rock.

I did eventually make a wax mould of my downstairs department thingy. It looked like . . . well, you know when you clean out the vegetable rack and you find a six-month-old carrot which has dried up and shrivelled? It was sad and took many years to get over.

I was still under the plaster mould in the BBC special effects department in Acton. This state of affairs seemed to go on for hours. My ears strained for any sound, but I couldn't hear anyone. I imagined that Peter Wragg and Bethan Jones and the lads had all gone out into the sunshine, they were sitting on the step, smoking, drinking tea, reading the papers and chatting about football. I imagined Peter Wragg saying, 'We could go down the pub if you like, we've got to wait a couple of hours for it to come off, not much we can do really.'

Suddenly there was a cracking sound, a deafening creaking wrenching noise, as if the very bowels of the earth were being ripped asunder. I felt my head move, not much, just a judder, and then the pressure on my face was suddenly gone. After a little more creaking there was a huge relief on my neck, the enormous weight of the back half of the mould was lifted away, and I could hear.

'Tip your head forward, Robert,' said Peter Wragg. 'We'll ease the mask off slowly then. Wriggle your face a bit.'

I did as I was told and slowly the mask moved. I could see light again, the minty lump was dragged from my mouth and I emerged back into the real world.

'That wasn't too bad, was it?' said Bethan Jones with her jaunty Welsh accent. Not too bad in comparison to being Hilti gunned★ to the underside of a battle tank on manoeuvres through a bramble patch at top speed. That's what I thought. What I said of course was, 'No, it was fine.' I said that because I'm a well-brought-up person, or, as Craig would say, a softy middle-class bastard.

They peeled the bald cap off and I had a wash, rubbing life back into my face. I returned to the casting room to see a plaster cast of my head emerging from the mould. It looked like the head of some sort of plug-ugly alien with bad posture. My neck had collapsed under the weight, my head was shunted forward so far I looked like a hungry giraffe. I couldn't believe it was me, I had a sideways nose, a double chin and a bumpy head.

There was another warning light on the control panel in the sky, and the small print beneath it read, IT'S NOT OVER YET. Next I had to stand in between two supports, on which I rested my arms, and have a body cast. This is where the whole torso and upper-arm area of the victim is wrapped in plastic cling film, then covered in plaster bandage up to a weight

★ For those not familiar with a Hilti gun, it is a tool used in the building trade to drive nails into solid concrete or brick with the aid of a small explosive charge.

19

of seven tons. It is not an intellectually stressful task. You have to stand up, stay still and shut up. I could do the first two, but the last I have always found impossible. I was moaning and complaining as the plaster overcoat got heavier and heavier and my feet started hurting.

If you've never stood absolutely still for a long time, it's difficult to imagine how something so simple could be so bloody uncomfortable. When you wait for a bus, or stand looking at a painting, as I'm sure you do very often, you are actually flitting about like a bird. Constantly shifting your weight from one foot to the other, scratching your bum and tapping your feet about. When you have to stand still, not move a muscle, it takes about forty seconds before you become uncomfortable, three minutes to be internally whinging, and after twenty minutes you can bore anyone to death with your list of complaints.

I'd learned this many years before when a friend talked me into posing in her life-drawing class. I had to stand in funny positions without a stitch on so that a lot of quite normal-looking people could draw my bits. Well, OK, they usually drew the rest of me first, but I was convinced they were really interested in my bits. After only a few moments what had started out as a very comfortable pose would become agony, and it was always made worse when the teacher said, 'Only another thirty-five minutes.' They liked draw-ing me because I was so thin in those days it was almost like drawing the human skeleton. Their other favourite model at the time was the opposite, Mr Lard Mountain they called him. I never met him, but I saw the drawings. He was big, I mean fat big, but also big big. He was big *everywhere*. All their drawings corroborated this. It made me very depressed. I was twenty-one, and that sort of thing is of prime importance then.*

Back in the BBC special effects department in Acton, Peter Wragg calmly kept applying bandage, smoothing it in and building up odd little ridges which would help when it had set and he'd remove it.

The relief when this great lump of stuff came off was immense. I felt as light as a feather, but was again depressed at the sight of this pot-bellied hunchback torso, that in my mind was a lightweight version of Arnold Schwarzenegger. After having my hands moulded, which was the least difficult, and being measured to bits, I was allowed to go. Surprisingly enough, looking back, I still really had no idea what I was letting myself in for.

* Not now of course.

CHAPTER 2

Just around the back from the BBC special effects department in Acton are the BBC rehearsal rooms. You can see them clearly if you drive down the A40, a big yellowish tower block which dominates the surrounding semi-industrial flat lands and cemeteries. *Red Dwarf* was on the fifth floor with the cast from *Blackadder* on one side of us and *You Rang M'Lord?* on the other. Alexei Sayle was down below us, and Jim Davidson was somewhere, I think, or was it Jimmy Tarbuck, and Paul Daniels and his wife. Oh it was marvellous. A thespian village transformed into a tower block. I took the lift to the fifth floor and found my way to our room. There was a little blackboard outside the door, and written in chalk it said RED DWARF III, DIRECTOR, ED BYE, PRODUCER, PAUL JACKSON.

I pushed open the double door and saw that I must have been very late as there were about twenty people sitting round a big table in the middle of a vast room. I wasn't intimidated, I'm an actor. I said hello in a high-pitched nervous voice and tried to find somewhere to sit. I was introduced to so many people it was hopeless. There was no way I would remember all these people I was going to be working with for the next ten weeks. Some of them I recognized: Bethan Jones from make-up, Peter Wragg from special effects, Rob and Doug, Ed Bye. And there was Hattie Hayridge whom I'd known for ages; we did stand-up comedy gigs together.

I shook hands with Chris Barrie. 'How d'you do, sir,' he said in a fairly formal manner. I shook hands with Danny John Jules. 'Yeah, how's it hangin', guy,' he said with a big grin. I shook hands with Craig Charles. 'What are you lookin' at, you middle-class bastard?' No, I lie, he didn't say that then, that wasn't until I'd been there a week. He said something like, 'Nice to have you on board,' and he bowed very low. Hattie looked very glamorous and settled, as if she'd been there for weeks. 'Hello, Hattie,' I said nervously and tried to sit near her.

In the middle of the table was a big pile of scripts. We were at the read-through, the first time each series when Rob and Doug get to hear the cast saying their words.

Chris and Craig are such good sight-readers, and Hattie too was very good. Danny has a unique style when he first reads a script. He seems to be scanning through different pages from everyone else, sometimes he's even looking through a different script. Sometimes he's not even looking at the script, he's reading about how much Pavarotti earns in a newspaper. It gets to his line and the room falls silent for a moment, Danny looks around with a big grin on his face. He's happy.

'Danny, it's your line, man,' says Craig.

'What?' says Danny.

'It's your line, man.'

'Page thirty-two, Dan,' says Chris.

'Oh yeah,' says Danny, finding the page. He clears his throat and says his line, which is: 'What's happening!'

Everybody laughs a great deal and the reading continues. The first time this happened Hattie and I were out of the picture. We didn't understand the long history Danny already had with the company. It would appear to the casual observer that Danny had no idea what was going on, he would smile and look around when it was his cue and Craig would do his line for him. Then put him in front of an audience and he is always on cue, always getting the laugh or, as Danny would say, 'Kicking comedy booty, guy.'

I read terribly that first day. I suddenly felt completely out of my depth. I was sitting around a table with a group of people who all knew each other well and who had been working in television for years. I had been working as a performer for years, but only with limited experience of TV.

I wasn't even playing a human, I was playing a mechanoid called Kryten. I didn't know what he was supposed to be, what he looked like, where he'd come from, why he was there. I didn't know anything. I'd never seen the episode in the second series where Kryten first appeared. At that time Kryten was played by David Ross who later became Talkie Toaster and who also put in a magnificent performance as the headmaster in Alan Bleasdale's *GBH*. I read Kryten in my own voice, and what were very funny lines came out about as amusing as dog pooh. At the end of a marathon session, six half-hour scripts, all of which took longer than that to read, it was hard for me not to be a little despondent. It seemed like such a mammoth task ahead. All these thousands of words to learn, and I hadn't written them.

This was the part that was so different for me. I had spent the previous ten years learning lines almost as I had written them. I had written everything I had ever performed except once: a play at the Sheffield Crucible called *The True Story of the Titanic*.

I played about six different characters, had loads of lines to learn which were written by someone else, and I found it very hard. The director was Stephen Daldry, a scruffy git in those days, though now he's gone all posh and runs the Royal Court in London. I keep seeing him now on telly, winning awards for amazing plays he's directed; he dresses very smartly and has nice haircuts. But when he was trying to get me to do a dance piece and say lines at the same time, his abilities in coaxing a performance out of an actor were stretched to the limit. To give myself a small break, I never blew it in a performance though. In that respect I'm like Danny; give me an audience and I can remember things my day-to-day brain would find utterly incomprehensible.

The play in Sheffield was performed by what I refer to as proper actors: people who've been to drama school and done proper acting training. They have learned how to absorb lines, learned stagecraft, understand music and dance, and can do proper singing. The cast of *Red Dwarf* are not proper actors in those terms. I came out of the alternative comedy brigade of the late seventies and early eighties. Craig Charles started life as a performance poet. Chris Barrie I first saw doing impressions in a late-night comedy club. Hattie does devastatingly funny deadpan comedy routines. Danny was in *Cats*, *Starlight Express* and loads of other musicals as a dancer.

That was my problem. Before going to the read-through, I had reassured myself that I was working with a group of people who were more like me, not proper actors but renegade comics who wouldn't be able to read scripts well the first time. I was very wrong.

As soon as the read-through was over, everyone got up and started talking to each other. I went to the special BBC tea table which all those rehearsal rooms have. As I was making myself some tea, Bethan Jones asked me if it would be all right to try my head on, as the first mask was ready. I agreed.

Rob and Doug came up to me and we talked about what Kryten should sound like. I said that I didn't want him to be English because he was bound to sound like R2D2. Or was it C3PO? Anyway, the humanoid one who said, 'Oh no, Master Luke!' all the time. It would be so easy to say, 'Oh no, Master Dave!' and end up having a totally unoriginal robot on your hands. Rob smiled and smoked, Doug walked in little circles nodding and saying, 'Yeah, yeah, yeah, no.'

'What about a walk?' said Rob. The walk. The moment I'd been dreading. When I first met Rob and Doug, weeks before, they'd been sitting down behind a table. I showed them my full range of comedy walks, which they seemed to admire. By the time of the read-through, I knew Doug had a false leg, due to an accident when he was a kid. His walk is obviously affected by this, so my desire to do a comedy wobbly robo-walk was somewhat hampered. I had done a great many comedy walks in my time. In fact, one kind reviewer had once written, '. . . Llewellyn's funny walks put John Cleese to shame . . .' Well, I never like reviews which compare one performer with another, and they certainly didn't put John Cleese to shame. I mean, let's face it, had John Cleese been in the audience that night I don't think he'd have got up out of his seat after seeing my funny walk and said, 'That's it, I'll never perform again, I feel put to shame!'

My lack of desire to start comedy walking certainly wasn't Doug's fault: it was painfully clear that he didn't give a toss about it. It was all my own inner middle-class guilt-ridden rubbish getting in the way. The big problem with comedy walks is that they invariably mimic someone who is disabled in some way. It's a problem with a lot of character comedy: you are often imitating someone who isn't 'normal'

27

in the dull, grey sense of the word. You are being some-one who is a bit bonkers, or a tosser, or a sad old git. But comedy walks have a specific danger all of their own.

Once when I was on tour with the comedy group The Joeys at a theatre in Swansea I did my Douglas Bader walk to pass the time and keep up the morale of my co-performers. Bader, who of course had lost both his legs in plane crashes, had a very specific walk. It's the only way you *can* walk if you keep both knees straight and don't flex your ankles. You have to get all your movement from your lower back and pelvic girdle. A lot of men don't think they've got a pelvic girdle, they think a girdle is a girly thing. But we do have them, which proves that all men are a bit girly anyway.

So there I was, doing my Douglas Bader walk across the stage. My fellow-performers and road man-ager were egging me on, thinking it was all terribly clever and funny, then a charming old man came in at the back of the theatre and stood still for a moment. He called out, 'Would you like some tea?' We waved and said we'd love some, then I watched in horror as this man turned with great difficulty and walked out. He did a Douglas Bader walk: he had two false legs. He'd been watching me do my funny walk probably thinking I was taking the piss. I felt, well, let's say I flew over the pit of utter shame in a hang-glider with no canvas.

Pulling faces, or girning, can be a dangerous occupation as well. Another kind reviewer once said,

'. . . Llewellyn's facial gymnastics have to be seen to be believed . . .' I liked that one, facial gymnastics, nice one. Had that one put on the poster, I can tell you. But there is a downside to facial gymnastics as well.

In one Joeys show there was a sketch about the Law Lords. It implied Britain's top judges were like mummified relics from a bygone age. I played the mummy, which involved funny walks and a great deal of highly energetic facial gymnastics. One night, in Canterbury I think, we had a brilliant audience, half of which came from a local special school. They were amazing, loving every minute of the show and screaming for more. However, there was one guy in the front row who didn't have a lot of control of his face and when I walked forward, playing the judge, I noticed him looking at me. As a three-thousand-year-old mummified judge I was distorting my face in a way unnervingly similar to him. I felt terrible, then he burst out laughing and pointed at me.

It's a difficult area and one I'm useless at. I always seem to blow it by trying to be too careful. In fact, the year *Mammon* was running in Edinburgh I met a wonderful man called Jag Plah. Jag is an Indian stand-up comic who can only just stand up: he has been disabled from birth. He stumbles on to a stage, which takes some time, and advises the audience to talk amongst themselves while he gets to the microphone. He then grabs the mike stand and drops his crutches. He looks at them lying on the floor and says, 'Look at that, they're useless without me.'

I learned a great deal from being with Jag, one of the main things being that if you ignore someone's disability, you're not being honest with them. He would always confront able-bodied people's discomfort head on. We once went out to eat in a restaurant in Edinburgh which had a steep flight of steps to the entrance. As we were leaving a young Canadian couple in tartan shirts were waiting to go in. As soon as they realized Jag was on crutches they looked away, I suppose in the belief that they might have embarrassed him with their stares. I could suddenly see what it must be like to be studiously ignored by everyone who sees you. Jag responded by saying, 'Stand back, crip coming.'

When Jag spoke, or walked, it was clear that it was more effort for him than most other people. In most other respects Jag was a bog-standard egotistical stand-up comic. One difference was that he didn't drink. He claimed in his comedy routine that if he drank alcohol he felt completely legless.

I should have been super cool about Doug's leg, but I didn't know him then and felt very uncomfortable. I decided to go for broke though and suggested I could base Kryten's walk on a kid I was at school with. He had muscular dystrophy, a wasting nerve disease, but at the age of fifteen he was still able to walk. He was the hero of our class mainly because he was so funny. Kids can be really horrible about that sort of thing, but for some reason our class had really taken this boy under its wing. If he answered a teacher's question he would put his hand up by swinging his shoulders and flicking his arm up, then holding his elbow with the other hand. This style of attracting the teacher's attention quickly caught on and soon we were all doing it. I think it had a beneficial influence on the whole class: we were the bad lads of the school, in the problem class, but because putting your hand up to answer a question was such fun, we started to pay more attention. This boy's walk was also very peculiar: he would flick his legs forward with a twist of his hips, sort of like Douglas Bader with rubber knees. When I perambulated across the floor like this for Rob and Doug they clearly liked what they saw. Doug walked around in a circle, nodding and saying, 'No, no, yeah, no, yeah.' Rob smoked another five cigarettes and said, 'Very funny, Bobby.'

Ed Bye wanted to know what sort of voice I was going to use. I searched my brains for all the daft comic characters I'd done over the years: Toby, the chinless wonder upper-class twit with buck teeth; Sir George Sprout, the gout-ridden old landowner; the boy Tom, ancient rustic know-all; Steve Crèche Ponytail, the massively right-on non-sexist man. None of them fitted the bill.

I tried my Dutch hippie accent, then I did my Scandinavian. It was a character I'd used in my stand-up comedy set who talked about having sex on a beanbag in a stripped-pine living room with a Janis Joplin poster on the wall. The accent has a daft singsong quality to it, a charming innocence or stupidity, depending on your viewpoint. As I did the walk and the voice, the general consensus seemed to be settling on Kryten being a Swedish mechanoid. Very clean and tidy, very Swedish, a sort of Volvo robot with side-impact bars.

It felt good, I seemed to have cracked it, then Rob and Doug started walking around, standing in a huddle, smoking and talking. I didn't really notice this, I was busy perfecting my walk, watching myself in the large mirror attached to one wall. Just as the character was starting to work for me, Rob walked up and said, 'The Scandinavian stuff.'

I said, 'Yeah, it really feels good.'

'No,' said Rob, 'it's going to drive people insane. That voice really gets to you after a while. What about American?'

'Yeah, American, no, yeah, yeah,' said Doug. That was OK, I had spent time in America, it made more sense in some ways, a robot was far more likely to come from America than Sweden. You can see how strongly I held on to my opinions, I don't swim with the tide, I stick to my beliefs, sometimes, for a bit, as long as everyone likes me.

I did my Californian, my bland Midwest, they were all a bit dull. Then I explained I'd spent time in Vancouver a few years before, having sex with a blonde Canadian woman in funny positions in various natural woodland settings. Not that the sex was import-ant to the accent, although her accent was great. It was a sort of American Swedish. Canadians have a similar singsong quality, and West-coast Canadians have a very particular vowel sound. The best-known proponent of this accent in Britain is Loyd Grossman, who can twist vowels the rest of us didn't know existed.

I tried the walk again, now with the distorted Canadian accent, 'Eouo, helleo thar Mustur Dayvid Suur, Iy hayve youuour breakfust, just as yououo orduered it.'

That was it. Kryten, as I portray him, was born at that moment. Obviously when I finally had the whole costume on the walk changed, the arm movements were defined by what I could and couldn't do, but the voice is more or less the same.

However, there is no rest for the egotistical, and no sooner was I riding the crest of a comedy wave in the rehearsal room than Bethan Jones led me into the little side room, sat me on a chair and slicked back my hair. This is the first stage in the make-up procedure, and I was having the first test of Kryten's head.

Next came the bald cap, like a thin bathing cap, which is stuck to the skin with spirit gum all around the hairline to hold it in place. Then, the worst bit, the mask, a one-piece moulded Balaclava of latex foam, was pulled over my head like a giant split condom. First, they glued the rear section on to the back of my head. Then, starting with the forehead, they glued the mask to my face. Glue all over my nose, cheeks, lips, chin, neck and ears. In fact, more or less everywhere except my eyelids.

I looked in a mirror and saw a very odd spectacle. The mask was unpainted and looked the same colour as a Band-Aid you'd find floating in a swimming-pool. A sort of dirty grey-beige colour. The skin around my eyes looked very dark, so I could still, as it were, see myself under the rubber. Rob, Ed and Doug came in and stood around looking at it. Bethan Jones explained to them all about the mask's difficulties. Rob smiled and smoked. Doug said, 'Yeah, great, yeah, yeah.' Ed Bye said, 'Well, chap, what's it like?'

I don't know what I said. I think we discussed the theory of irony. I said that it was ironic how when I'd first met them I was worried about being recognized for being a robot, worried about getting typecast. Here I was, so well covered in prosthetic foam even my own mother wouldn't recognize me.

After about twenty minutes Bethan Jones removed the mask and I was back to normal. Even that early on there was a huge relief that washed over me when the thing finally came off. I washed my face and felt it carefully with my hands. It felt new and different, even after such a short time. I made a mental note of the amount of days I had before the next mask was being applied ready for the first day's filming, which was to take place in Liverpool.

CHAPTER 3

The beginning of recording the third series of *Red Dwarf* was a difficult time for me because I was already committed to performing in a new play I had co-written, to be premièred at the Edinburgh Festival, 1989. The play was called *Onan*. It was an idea I had been knocking around for a long time, and it finally came to fruition when I co-wrote it with John McKay.

Onan was the story of two men who set up the first non-sexist, non-racist, right-on pornographic magazine. The magazine was called *Onan*, named after the biblical figure who spilled his seed on the ground. I discovered you can say 'spilled his seed' on radio and television, but if you say 'wanker' people seem to get upset. Funny old world. Anyway, the play dealt with all the thorny issues surrounding the production and consumption of pornography, but it dealt with them in a humorous and witty way. We hoped.

When I wasn't doing read-throughs and costume fittings for *Red Dwarf*, I was busy rehearsing *Onan* in an old school building in Hackney.

John and I both appeared in the play, and our first-night try-out took place in the Soho Poly theatre in London. Considering it was a comedy the laughs were few and far between. It felt very leaden and worthy, the audience were crammed into their seats in the tiny basement theatre. Afterwards John and I were both pretty depressed. We had both had successful shows the previous year in Edinburgh, now we were going up with what felt like a bit of a dog.

Everyone who saw the show in London was very nice about it. 'It's fantastic, guys, it really says a lot,' said someone who looked faintly bored. 'I really laughed,' said someone else without cracking a smile. We were also in a bit of trouble because in the normal course of events we'd have had time to jiggle the play around a bit, between the first performance and our arrival in Edinburgh. Now, due to my filming schedule, this wasn't possible. The day after this glamour-free première, I drove to Liverpool and checked in at the hotel.

I was greeted in the bar by the full complement of *Red Dwarf*: the sound men, the cameramen, the vision mixers, lighting technicians, boom operators, the rest of the cast, Rob and Doug. The whole lot of us took over the corner bar of the hotel. Craig walked in and was greeted at every table he passed. Everyone in Liverpool knew Craig, and he implied to me that half the people who knew him wanted to kill him, so I moved myself slightly further away.

We all went out for a meal, which, considering there were about eighty people in all, took hours of careful organization. Craig and Danny then went off clubbing. I had to go to bed. This is the story of my life, everyone else goes off clubbing, I go to bed.

The reason I went to bed was made apparent in the dark hours of early morning. My bedside phone went, I answered it, a Liverpudlian woman's voice said, 'This is your early morning call, Mr Llewellyn.' It had started, this was my first day proper on *Red Dwarf*.

Half an hour later I was sitting in a make-up chair in the temporary BBC Liverpool studios, which were on the site of the Liverpool Garden Festival, which was on the site of the old docks, which were on the site of the older docks, which were on the site of a forest probably. Nothing is permanent on earth, nothing can be conserved, change is the only constant. There we go, that's the sort of paper-thin philosophy I filled my head with as I sat watching Bethan Jones and Gill put my make-up on.

This first day I sat in the make-up chair for something like six hours. They were trying it out, testing different colours and powders, painting the mask once it was stuck on me. I'll say it just once because it's boring, but the masks are extremely uncomfortable to wear. It's hard to describe, and I've tried to do it many times. I've said things like, It's like wearing someone else's old socks over your face all day, with a local anaesthetic, like a dentist gives you, and then sitting in a sauna. It's also like having mud slapped on your face and then dried so it goes all tight. What it's really like is having your whole head covered with prosthetic foam rubber. There is no way of knowing without doing it. It is hot, it is uncomfortable, it does make me a bit irritable, in fact I'm a bit irritable now, writing about it. Just leave me alone will you, don't stand so close. Get off my case. Jesus!

OK, there, that's it, I'll really try not to go on about the mask. It may pop up occasionally, but I'll try and keep it to a minimum.

I'll never forget that first day as long as I live. The irony warning light was on red alert. After six hours in make-up, I finally stood up and stretched the stretch of the un-dead. I had a hyper stretch since my buttocks were as numb as a monk's cassock tassle, as they say in Australia.

I went into the costume department and was met by the lanky form of Howard Burden, the genius behind all the *Red Dwarf* cossies. I have to admit there have been times, maybe as a shard of fibreglass has wormed its way into my anatomy, or my shoulders have ached because of the armour I'm wearing, or when my core body temperature has gone so high I've seen Russian helicopters hovering above me ready to pour sand on my head, that I have been known to call Howard things other than a genius. But it's all done with great love and understanding because what you see works very well, and, as we troopers in showbiz always say, 'that's what's important.'

Actually, that's bull, what we really say is, I really can't work in this cossie, love, it's sheer agony! On the first day I got zipped, buckled, popped, riveted, Velcroed and strapped into my costume. For three or four minutes it was very comfortable, then I tried to sit down and my plastizote buttocks came flying off. I walked around in it for a while, visited the set where Craig was filming. It was incredible: the remains of a crashed spaceship could be seen stranded on top of an iceberg. It was all made of polystyrene and bits of old hardboard, but it looked great. They were filming the inserts for the episode titled *Marooned*. Craig was stumbling about in the snow, being buffeted by a howling blizzard. This was created by an old Volkswagen car engine on a stand, attached to a gigantic propeller. It can create enough wind to blow you off your feet. It worked, Craig went flying very effectively. He was only too willing to do his own stunts.

'Hey, Ed, how about I come out of the door and dive out,' said Craig, wiping the fake snow from his hair, 'and you know, like, land on me head? That'd look good.'

'Yes,' said Ed brightly, 'and you'd also be dead, which would leave me looking like a right wally.'

'Hey, Eddy, man,' said Craig, 'I can land on me head and no harm done. I'm a Scouser man, you know what I'm saying?'

'Yes, I know exactly what you're saying, and you're completely mad.'

Just as the wind machine was getting ready to blow Craig through the supporting wall of the studio, lunch was called. Another bit of standard *Red Dwarf* irony. I had spent six and a half hours getting ready, and then I had to sit still for an hour and do nothing while everyone had lunch. I don't blame people for having lunch, I think it is their most fundamental human right to have lunch. It's just ironic, or Sod's Law, that it always seems to happen that I am ready just before lunch. I went into the Portakabin that was my dressing room and sat down and looked in the mirror. The mask was extraordinary, it was impossible to see where the mask stopped and my face began. I looked at myself for a long time.

That moment was the one and only time I was terrified of Kryten. It was the shock of being alone, looking in a mirror and not seeing yourself looking back. Someone else, some square-headed dork with chiselled features, was looking back at me. I looked closer, it was someone else, it wasn't me there. My heart rate went off the scale, I felt dizzy and nauseous, I felt as if someone had spiked my tea with a harsh hallucinogenic drug. I was, as they say in Australia, off my face. I looked away from the mirror and tried to compose my thoughts, I really felt like I was going mad. I was very scared. I stood up, I had to get away from the mirror, but the movement of my standing caught my eye in the mirror and I looked back. There he was again, that bloke with no hair and a cuboid head. It was horrible.

I walked out of the Portakabin, through the makeshift dining area and into the parking-lot outside. I walked past people who were working on the show, technicians and office staff, and they all ignored me. They had no idea I'd just had the fright of my life.

They couldn't tell if I was happy or sad, or angry or upset, or scared even. To them, I was the poor sod in the rubber mask. It made me super aware of how much we can give away with our faces when we think people won't notice.

We are all, unconsciously most of the time, very good at reading people's faces; we can usually tell at a glance what sort of mood someone we know is in. If you remove that element, people start to cut you off, start to remove you from their mind's eye, take less notice of you. Is this what it is like being disabled or having a terrible facial disfigurement?

'Cretin,' said a voice with a French accent, 'do you want a cup of tea, Cretin?'

It was Sylvie, the company runner. She was a very small French woman who could not pronounce the name Kryten, and settled on Cretin, which means the same in French. She looked me in the eye when she asked me if I wanted tea, then she gently reached up and touched my rubber face. 'It must be very 'ot,' she said.

I nodded, it was very 'ot. I'd only been in it seven hours and I was parched. It was interesting that some people were not at all intimidated by the mask, and some were so horrified that they looked away.

Sylvie's radio crackled into life, asking her to go into the studio. She replied, 'I am making tea for Cretin,' which meant the whole crew heard her call me Cretin. It was naturally only a matter of time before the rest of the cast were calling me Cretin, especially Danny who found it peculiarly amusing. Danny's laugh could easily win the international full-bodied-laugh grand prix.

I got a cup of tea from Sylvie and then found I couldn't drink it. It was like trying to drink after you've been to the dentist and your lips are completely numb. I couldn't feel my own lips, but immediately the tea touched my prosthetic lips they absorbed the fluid and tasted like I was sucking someone else's flannel in the bath. Did you ever do that as a kid, suck your flannel? I did. My mum was always telling me not to, but at least it was my own flannel. I have no idea why I did it. But imagine doing that, thinking it was your flannel and feeling quite happy about it, and then realizing it was someone else's flannel.

Lunch was supplied by location caterers, my favourite form of eating. I will often agree to doing a job if I hear the production is being made on location. It means one of those big trucks will be there with the two men in white who serve amazing food in the middle of nowhere.

Here's a tip. If you see a film crew near your street, try and beg, borrow or steal a windproof jacket, get a peak cap with the name of a TV show or film on the front, and join the queue. The food is free and very nice. If anyone asks who you are, which is very unlikely, tell them you're from a company with a TV-type name, something like Telly Techno or Telly Graphic, and you're on set to talk to Nick. There is always a technician called Nick on every crew. I've done this many times around North London. Of course it does help if you know one of the lighting or sound people, but I have managed to get a free lunch from location productions where I didn't know a soul.

There was a long queue leading up to the step of the location catering truck. I was salivating, I'd missed breakfast, I'd been sitting still for hours, my body was pleading with me for some form of low-level pleasure. Food, anything, an old carrot, just something different from the stifling tightness.

I chose the roast beef, with the cauliflower, peas and roast potatoes. I made my way from the truck to the double-decker bus that doubles as a dining room. I sat down and looked at this plate of food. How on earth was I going to get it into my mouth?

I chopped everything up small and tried to get it past my lips without touching them. My prosthetic lips tasted so horrible by now I didn't want them to spoil my lunch. I soon found that by tipping my head backwards, I could more or less drop food into my open mouth from above. After I had done this a few times, I looked up and saw Craig looking at me sympathetically. 'You poor sod,' he said. I did feel pretty miserable. I stopped eating before I finished my food and stared at what remained, sadly.

'Cretin, they want you in wardrobe,' said Sylvie, so that was it. I couldn't really eat. After slipping into my costume (I use the term slipping in a comedy way) I had to go to make-up again to be touched up before going on the set.

'You've ruined your lips!' said Bethan Jones, viewing the damage all that tea and gravy had done. I was there another thirty minutes being re-glued, repaired and powdered, then, finally, I entered the studio to do my first shot for *Red Dwarf*.

In the story, the Cat (Danny J. J.) was out searching for Lister and Rimmer on Starbug, which had crash-landed and was marooned on an ice planet. The Cat had harnessed Kryten to a sledge, and the scene demanded that I pull this sledge, with Danny and a load of provisions, across a snowy landscape in a blizzard. He had to shout 'Mush! Mush!' as if I were a pack of dogs, and lash me with a bullwhip. Danny loved this scene, but I was not so keen. For a start, when I was tied up to the sledge I couldn't get a grip in all the fake snow, so Peter Wragg tied another rope to the sledge and somehow managed to lie down on the floor and pull the sledge for me. That would have been cool, but then they brought round the wind machine, the one they'd been blowing Craig around with in the morning. To get a good blizzard effect, they would start up the wind machine and then pour Dreft soap flakes into the wind.

Ed arranged the camera and they started the wind machine. As soon as it was up to full blast, which was deafening, they started the blizzard effect. Within seconds, due to intense eye pain, I realized that my eye-blink ability was severely restricted. The make-up was so heavy around my eyes that I really couldn't close them. Super-painful shards of Dreft mild and gentle soap powder stung my forced-open eyeballs. I grimaced and tried to cover my face. I couldn't see or hear anything. I finally turned away from the shot and someone killed the wind machine. I looked at Danny through soap vision. He was sitting on the sledge, in a big fur coat. He was smiling from cheek to cheek and saying 'Mush! Mush!'

'No, the shot doesn't work, chaps,' said Ed Bye. Now there's irony for you. For the next hour or so, we tried various different combinations of me pulling the sledge through various mixtures of fake snow. All of these combinations involved Danny sitting on the sledge going 'Mush! Mush!' In the final broadcast version of *Marooned*, none, I repeat *none*, of these shots was used. I thought that warranted a special irony warning light on the giant heavenly dashboard, what I didn't see was the upcoming irony Klaxon horn, which was warning about the following day.

Now I have promised not to go on about the mask and the heat and discomfort, and I won't, but this day continues to hold the record for being the most ironic of all.

We moved to a hotel in Manchester, a very splendid place called the Midland. Not that I noticed its splendour much when I woke up. Five-thirty in the morning in Manchester is not a glamorous time, but what is glamour anyway? A fleeting feeling which leaves no trace. No, this had no glamour, sitting in the back of a taxi which smelt strongly of that special taxi air-freshener. The sort that's in the little cardboard holder that hangs from the rear-view mirror and feels as if it's peeling a layer of skin off your nostrils.

'Telly is it?' said the driver.

'Yah, actually it's a series called *Red Dwarf*, I play a robot,' I said, trying to sound like an actor.

'Never heard of it,' said the driver. He wiggled his way through the back streets of Manchester and dropped me by the side of the BBC's studios on Oxford Road.

I stumbled into the BBC building and headed for the canteen. I knew how hungry I was going to get so I thought I'd better stoke up. The canteen was shut. Irony warning light on orange. I went to the make-up room and sat down. The process which next took place I don't want to describe for two very good reasons. One, it's boring, and two, it brings it all back as I write it and I don't have my prosthetic counsellors★ here to help me.

Suffice it to say, six hours later I was laughing and joshing around in the costume department. I got changed into my costume and was then transported by cab to the Midland Hotel where we were recording in a gym. Irony warning light to darker orange.

In the episode called *Body Swap*, Lister and Rimmer

★ Prosthetic counsellors are specially trained psychologists who help actors who have suffered extensive full-face prosthetics in their lives. They first started research in this important area after members of the *Planet of the Apes* cast went barking mad.

had done a deal whereby Rimmer was allowed to have a go in Lister's body for a while. The scene we were recording was meant to show Rimmer exercising Lister's body by sitting in a Jacuzzi, reading a female body-builders' magazine and smoking a huge cigar. I entered with a huge selection of food for him to gorge himself on, and was then meant to light a candle with my finger and serve the food.

OK, by now the irony warning light was on red, but the Klaxon hadn't quite gone off. Had this been a US peace-keeping force as opposed to my irony control, the F111s would have been in the air, missiles armed and ready.

I noticed when I first arrived that the crew were all wearing shorts and T-shirts. 'Morning, Robert.' It was Peter Wragg standing next to me, holding a glove, a gas bottle and a lot of wires. He started to fit the glove on, run the wires and the gas tube up my sleeve and out behind my head. 'It's just an electric-spark cigarette lighter,' said Peter. 'Bog standard. We'll be back here, and on the cue we'll fire it up. A flame will come out of the end of your finger, you light the candle and blow the flame on your finger out, then we turn the gas off.'

'Great, that's fine, yeah,' I said, which is liberal speak for, Oh my God, I'm going to die but I don't want to be rude to this nice man.

Ed Bye was chirpy and happy as usual. 'All right, chap?' he said.

'Bit hot,' I said, and then felt guilty for complaining.

'It's bloody boiling in here,' said Ed. 'You must be roasting alive in there. This won't take long.'

Irony Klaxon horn sounding for the first time, just one blast, but I should have noticed. Craig came in, wearing a pair of swimmers and a dressing-gown, looking truly like the Crown Prince of Packet.*

'Hey, Krytie, you're looking good, man,' he said as he shed his dressing-gown and dropped into the pool. Craig was immediately in his element, looking at pictures of highly muscled, semi-naked women, smoking a cigar and lounging in a pool.

We went for a take. I had to push a trolley laden with food and not trip up over the wires and tubes strapped to my back. Craig was mouthing his lines, Chris would dub them on later. I had to guess when my cue was by watching his lips. Then I presented the food and went to light the candle.

Peter saw his cue and hit the button. A sharp jolt of pain shot up my arm, I jerked, then there was another. 'I'm being electrocuted!' I said, not noticing there was a flame coming out of my finger. I waved this flaming digit around for a moment, but it didn't seem to want to go out. I am going to die, I thought. I am going to burst into flames and die. Not while I'm trying to save a family in a burning building, not

---

* The Prince of Packet is a popular nickname for Mr Charles. This is due to the mildly shocking size of his lower member, or tummy banana, otherwise known as packet.

heroically, but while making a British comedy TV show. How ironic.

Peter Wragg saved my life by blowing the little flame out. The fact that he saved my life was a mixed blessing, I thought. It meant I was still covered from head to foot in rubber and plastic, standing in a sauna in a Manchester hotel, and we hadn't shot a thing.

'Don't worry, chaps,' said Ed Bye, 'it's only a rehearsal.'

After they had stripped me down, we worked out that I was sweating so much under my costume that I had shorted out the wires leading to the gas nozzle. We tried the shot six or seven times, each time I got an electric shock, or the gas didn't light, or I blew my lines because I talked over Craig, or the sound of the Jacuzzi was too much.

I eventually went a bit dizzy and was taken to the exit, where it was much cooler. I can remember Paul Jackson being there, the man who'd got me this job. He'd come to see how things were going. 'How's it going, Robert?' he said.

'It's fine,' I lied, 'I'm just a bit hot.'

I think if people could have seen my face at that time, I would have been made to lie down. It would have looked the colour of a baboon's arse. But it was Kryten's face that they saw, calm and smooth, kind and sympathetic, in a cuboid, novelty-condom sort of way.

The rest of that day is a bit hazy. What we discovered afterwards was that if a human body sweats that much, you not only lose water (I was drinking two big bottles of mineral water a day, and not urinating once), but you also start losing essential salts and mineral things. I don't know what happens medically but it means you feel dizzy and tired and a bit sick.

Of course the final irony of ironies was that none of this footage was ever used. The scene was rewritten and done in a studio. This is the sort of irony where you need to learn breathing exercises and chant little Buddhist mantras to yourself otherwise you go mad.

Bethan turned up the next day with a box of diarrhoea salts that you give little kids in Somalia when they've got the runs. Helps rehydrate them. I felt guilty because I thought I was depriving some poor kid in the desert, which is a classic self-centred, middle-class, guilt-ridden thing to think.

The next three days were spent in various locations around Manchester, filming inserts for *Backwards*. This included Chris Barrie and me walking backwards through the Piccadilly shopping arcade dressed as a mechanoid and a hologram, and an unimaginable amount of people utterly failed to notice us. You can see on the footage they used that most of the busy Tuesday morning shoppers were totally oblivious of the fact that they had just walked past two men, one who looked a bit like Captain Scarlet with an H stuck on his forehead, the other with a square rubber head and a shiny silver body, who was walking backwards. We had to walk backwards, and I didn't understand this at the time, because when the film was run backwards, we would be walking forwards and all the shoppers would be walking backwards.

After one of these long days, I went back to our hotel, where we'd done the make-up, got cleaned off, had a shower and drove to Edinburgh. That was a mistake because I was exhausted and couldn't really see, but being a soft, southern bastard, I thought, Manchester's in the North, so is Scotland, so Edinburgh can't be far.

As I drove for hour after sleepy hour along near-deserted A roads through the borders, often driving with my head out of the window to try and keep awake, I realized I was very wrong.

I got to the little flat I'd rented in Edinburgh at about two-thirty in the morning to be greeted with tea and toast from John McKay, my writing partner and co-actor in *Onan*. He filled me in on the gossip and told me what was happening with our show, which was due to open the following day.

CHAPTER 4

The run of *Onan* went extremely well, after a difficult start when the audience clearly didn't know if we were doing a comedy or a tragedy. Once we got into our stride, we flew through the season, got rave reviews, had lunch, stood in the bar and laughed like actors, which means throwing your head back and making a lot of noise. We didn't make any money even though we were sold out from day one, but it was fun, and I forgot all about rubber masks and time travel. I met Hattie every now and then. She was doing very late-night stand-up comedy in the same room as I was working in, but that was the only contact I had with *Red Dwarf*.

Then I got a bit of glamour. I mean, it's sad, isn't it, but every now and then a bit of glamour does wonders. After the final show of *Onan*, the audience cheered and clapped, we bowed, ran off stage like actors do, I changed, washed my face, ran out of the front door of the Assembly Rooms, got in a taxi, got taken to the airport and flew back to London. As the plane climbed and circled around Edinburgh I could clearly make out the Scott monument, Newtown, George Street and the Assembly Rooms. I could see the roof of the Assembly Rooms where I had climbed, illegally, with a lot of drunk comics, to watch the fireworks display.

Considering I have never lived in the City of Edinburgh, I have spent an enormous amount of time there over the years. I feel attached to the place. I can walk around the streets and look up at windows and remember, Ah, I had sex in that room once or Ah, that's where that party was where Jenny LeCoat fell on my head. Or, That's the pub where I met Jasper Carrott. It's sad really, isn't it, to admit that you have those sort of thoughts as you wander about?

I sat back in my seat and felt a bit glamorous, and a bit sad. I think glamour and sadness go together very well as an emotional cocktail, like loneliness and self-pity, or love and happiness. I was sad because I was leaving my girlfriend and a lot of my friends in Edinburgh, and now, as I flew south, it felt like such a sudden parting. I'd barely had time to say goodbye to John McKay, who I'd been working so closely with for the previous three months. Plus I was missing the last day of the Festival, where everyone walks around with a hangover and reminisces about what went on during the previous three weeks.

Plus I was missing the big benefit gig, on the last Sunday of the Festival. I had been involved in that for the previous four years or so. It was always a great show, more like a party for the performers, with the added benefit of a huge audience. In earlier years the benefits were for the Nicaragua Solidarity Campaign, but this year it was for the Terrence Higgins Trust. OK, it's easy to be critical of benefits and what they do, reviving flagging rock stars' careers etc., but for all the free publicity it gave to a lot of the performers, it did raise a fair-sized wodge of cash.

Anyway, I was missing all that as I sat thirty thousand feet up and tucked into my British Midland chilled chicken roll. The man in the seat in front of me turned around and asked me, 'Are you the bloke that was doing that play about porn?'

'Well, it wasn't about porn, as such,' I said defensively. 'It was about a couple of left-wing, right-on, non-sexist men who set up a pornographic magazine.'

'Yeah, the play about porn. Because it's already been done,' he said. 'Look at this.'

He handed me a copy of *Forum* magazine. 'That's really what you were talking about, isn't it?'

I flicked through the magazine. I'd never actually looked through *Forum* before. Don't get me wrong, I'm no porno virgin. I'd seen it all, I had to do the research for the play; the trouble was I started the research when I was thirteen. But *Forum* had never interested me, there weren't enough pictures for a start. I handed the magazine back to the guy and tried to sleep. Of course that was a bit futile as the flight is only forty minutes and we were coming in to land.

Red Dwarf rehearsals proper started the following day, in Acton. The first episode we recorded was *Marooned*, which meant that Hattie, Danny and I had virtually nothing to do. It's one of my favourite episodes, not just because I'm not in it,* I just think it has some of the funniest lines from the whole series in it.

> LISTER: Are you saying I've got a big bum?
> RIMMER: Big, it's like two badly parked Volkswagens.

Danny, Hattie and I spent quite a lot of time in the BBC canteen as Chris and Craig learned reams of lines. The BBC canteen is on the top floor of the building, and on any given day in here you can see the stars. Ahem. You can see a few actors who are in a few BBC sitcoms. The actors from *You Rang M'Lord?* are all dressed as if they are about to go and play golf, which is no doubt what they do. The people from *Blackadder* all look professionally depressed, which is probably how we all looked too, that being the trendy look for our generation.

During lunch break Craig and Chris would join us and we devised this thing called a luvvie-ometer which would sound when we spotted a major-league luvvie entering the room. Luvviedom is a very specific complaint that it is horrifyingly easy to catch, which is why the *Blackadder* and *Red Dwarf* actors appear so morose. A miserable countenance seems to be the best way to counteract luvvieness.

A luvvie is always pleased to see everybody, always up, always exhausted (i.e., working a lot), and always

---

* I can never really enjoy something I'm in.

has a string of anecdotes a mile long . . . which have
. . . beautifully timed pauses . . . and exquisitely timed
delivery. They also never have a point or a punch-line
at the end of their stories. Merely a raised eyebrow and
a knowing expression. At the end of a long and dull
anecdote is when most actors realize they need writers.

I know of very few performers who have never
been struck down with luvviedom at some time. I
know I've had it, try as I might to avoid it.

'Hello there, Robert, how are you?' says a very
nice floor manager I worked with a year before.

'Oh God,' I say, looking to the heavens, 'utterly
exhausted,' head shake. 'Really it's because I'm crap,'
stare at person and nod vigorously, 'I'm a crap actor,
I shouldn't be allowed in here.'

The nice floor manager knows the score and re-
sponds appropriately. 'You're a very funny actor, I
saw your show in Edinburgh, it was excellent.'

'Oh, that's very kind, but anyway, no, I'm shagged.
Utterly drained, but it's really nice to see you, how
are you? . . . Oh, there's Ben [Elton] I'd better say hi.'
Walk walk walk . . . 'Hi, Ben.'

'Do I know you?' says Ben Elton. 'Guards, take
this man away!'

No, that's not true, I don't know many famous
people, but I do know Ben Elton. Sort of. Well, can I
truly say I know anyone, do we even know ourselves?
Rarely. Anyway, Ben used to do his set before The
Joeys in salubrious gigs like Chats Palace in Hackney
and the Covent Garden Community Centre.

During our time at Acton, we would rehearse for three days, then have a technical run-through, which is when all the crew would watch. Then we'd climb aboard a coach to drive to Manchester, where we'd check into the Midland Hotel and I'd generally go to bed.*

Not so the rest of the cast. They would imbibe fermented vegetable products and discuss the issues of the day. On the rare occasions when I didn't have to get up the following morning at five-thirty, I would sit, with a long glass of mineral water, and join in the hectic banter.

'What's happenin', guy?' says Danny

'Goin' clubbin', man,' says Craig.

'Kicking,' says Danny.

'What are we drinking, chaps?' says Ed Bye.

'Mine's a Bud,' says Chris.

'I'll just have a mineral water, with lemon and ice,' I say.

'Wimp,' says Craig and jumps on me for no obvious reason. Suddenly three very smartly dressed black men would enter the hotel bar escorted by four or five drop-dead-beautiful women, and Craig and Danny would go off clubbing, which I assume has

---

* I used to love staying in posh hotels, having your own bit of soap and your own bathroom. It's a telling fact that after you've stayed in posh hotels a lot, the thrill wears off. Does this mean that if you were sent out into space, which would be so amazing, after the hundredth trip you'd be bored? I think it's possible

something to do with sex in interesting positions with people of a like mind, which is why they all joined a club.

There was one memorable occasion when I had already been woken by a rude alarm call, got semi-dressed, stumbled out of bed and into the lift, got out on the ground floor to be met by Craig and Danny who had just come back from clubbing, and seemed to have enjoyed themselves greatly.

Craig and Danny's energy never ceased to amaze me. If I'd stayed up all night drinking, dancing and doing other repetitive body movements in the close proximity of another person, I would need considerable medical attention for at least a week. This would have to be followed by a prolonged period of counselling, therapy and the love and understanding of my friends and family.

In the morning Craig would sit down on a make-up chair next to me, I'd ask him how he was, he'd take a puff on his cigarette and say, 'Bit rough, man.' A bit rough! If I'd done what he'd done I'd be dead!

Our two days in Manchester were pretty intense. The first day in the studio was where we pre-recorded all the complicated technical stuff, the second day was spent rehearsing with the cameramen and sound crew, and then recording the remainder of the show in front of a live audience.

A live audience. It never occurred to me to be nervous about this. I had spent the previous ten years in front of live audiences virtually every night of the week, but they weren't live *Red Dwarf* audiences. As I entered the back of the studio in Manchester for my first live *Red Dwarf* recording, the buzz from the audience was extraordinary.

Paul Jackson* went out to warm them up, which was a bit like warming up a car that has just driven a hundred miles. This audience was running hot. Paul cracked a few rude jokes and we were introduced one by one.

'Ladies and gentlemen, as Rimmer, Mr Chris Barrie.' Huge deafening applause, whistling, whooping.

'Ladies and gentlemen, as Lister, Mr Craig Charles.' Stupendous hysterical rapture.

'Ladies and gentlemen, as the Cat . . .' No more could be heard as Danny pirouetted into view.

'As Holly the computer, please welcome Hattie Hayridge.' Very interested polite clapping, with the semi-audible audience thought of, Oooh, so that's what the new Holly looks like.

'As Kryten the mechanoid, Mr Robert Llewellyn.' Polite smattering of semi-supportive clapping. The audience thinking, Bloody hell, what does he look like?

The recording took place, the warm-up man kept the audience from flagging between takes. Every week Craig would walk up to this man, take the microphone from him and say to the audience, 'You

* Still the producer at this time.

know who this guy is, don't you?' The man would buckle over in dramatic embarrassment. 'You know who he is, I'll tell you, he's Ronald McDonald. He's the bloke in that fucking clown outfit!'

After the recording I would head straight to make-up, while everyone else headed straight for the bar. By the time I was stripped, oiled, pummelled, powdered and cleaned off, I would run to the bar just in time for a quick orange juice before getting into the bus and heading back to London.

The journey back was often very rowdy, since everyone except Mike Agnew the floor manager was high from doing the show. Mike would have worked so absurdly hard for the previous two days that he would flop down on the long back seat of the bus and be completely oblivious of the noise surrounding him. We would have videos of *Star Trek* playing, Craig would be roaming the coach looking for cigarettes, cans of beer or trouble, and Danny would be holding court about how much Pavarotti earned.

'For just one night, guy,' he would say dramatically, holding your gaze, then suddenly, 'just one night the geezer has to sing, and he doesn't get a fee, guy. They don't give him no fee. They give the man a cheque-book and say, write out however much you want, Mr Pavarotti, sir. I tell you, that man makes serious money.'

'What you on about, Dan?' says Craig who appears from the seat behind.

'Danny's just filling us in on the facts behind

Pavarotti's bank balance,' says Chris, 'and very interesting it is too, sir.'

'You're not still on about Pavarotti, are you, Dan?'

'I tell you, guy,' says Dan, now seriously warming to his subject, 'he doesn't get paid in money, he gets paid in bullion.'

'What planet d'you live on, Dan?' asks Craig, reaching across to get a can of wicked-strength lager.

'Bullion, man, he doesn't have a wallet, he gets followed around by a Securicor van full of his spending bullion.'

'I don't expect all that money makes him happy though, Dan,' I say.

'Bollocks, man,' says Craig, 'it would make me happy.'

'He is seriously rich, guy, I'm tellin' you.'

'I believe you, Dan,' says Chris. 'I'm perfectly prepared to believe the man earns some serious money.'

'Not as much as you though, Chris,' says Craig, laughing through his teeth.

'Well, I'm not prepared to say,' says Chris.

'No, but you do earn a lot of money, Chris,' says Craig. No comment from Chris.

'You bought that Bentley last year.'

'A Bentley! Did you really buy a Bentley, Chris, man?' asks Danny.

'I'm afraid I did, sir,' says Chris.

'That is a serious poom-poom wagon,' says Danny. I am lost now, I have no idea what a poom-poom wagon is. Danny finds this very amusing.

'He don't know what a poom-poom wagon is, guy,' says Danny to Craig.

'Where have you been, Robert, man, with all your poxy Oxbridge mates? A poom-poom wagon is a car that you get a bit of poom poom in,' says Craig, making various gestures with his arms and central torso area which indicate sexual intercourse.

'Oh, right, with you,' I say, trying to be hip. Failing miserably.

'A Bentley, man,' says Danny. 'That is serious executive poom-poom material.'

The concept of executive poom poom was clearly beyond anything Craig would tolerate. 'Danny, you really are totally out of order, man.'

'I must say, Dan,' said Chris jocularly, 'I have never seen the Bentley in terms of its poom poomness, but now you mention it you may well have a point.'

'I'm tellin' you, guy, you could get some serious poom poom if you cruise around in that motor, you know what I'm saying? A Bentley.'

Conversations not unlike these, in fact horrifyingly like these, would pass the miles between Manchester and London like syrup of figs helps you pass solids. Most of the time the talk would take place around Rob and/or Doug, and it is only now, looking back, that it becomes clear how one of the interesting developments in *Red Dwarf* has taken place in the four years I have been involved with it.

Slowly but surely we have each either grown like

our characters or our characters have grown something like us. This is not to say that Chris Barrie is a git like Rimmer, far from it, but there are *elements* of Chris in the character. It's also, I hasten to add, not to say I am like a mechanoid, with nothing down there except plastic underpants and a trade mark. But I do tend to do a lot of laundry and washing-up at home. Craig and Danny also have many traits of their characters, and I'm sure that as Rob and Doug got to know us better, and listened to us talking on the coach, more and more of our own personalities, neuroses and character traits started being incorporated into the script.

At something like three in the morning the coach would pull up in the car park of the Acton rehearsal rooms. What a place to be at three in the morning. Very low glamour rating. We would fall out of the bus and climb into a veritable fleet of waiting taxis lined up in the road.

I would hit my pillow at about four, still peeling bits of rubber from my chin and neck, but as I slipped into slumber town, I would glow with happiness. It was another five days without the mask, and one whole day off.

The following week I arrived as usual at Acton, we read the script through, I was feeling more at home, I had more to do in the episode, and things were generally looking up. Irony warning signal on low.

The episode we were recording was called *Polymorph*, a deadly creature that could turn into anything.

It slowly became clear during the course of the day that at some time it was going to turn into a snake.

Donna DiStefano, our long-suffering assistant floor manager, asked me discreetly if I was scared of snakes. I told her I wasn't, I was a bit scared of really big spiders, but snakes were fine. She nodded, and smiled. Why didn't I realize at the time? Why didn't I realize that Donna knew something I didn't?

The week's rehearsals went well. Craig and I enjoyed a scene we did together when the polymorph turned into a pair of boxer shorts, which Craig put on and which then started to shrink. I had to try and pull them off, while still having a vacuum-cleaner hose attached to my groinal socket, at which point Rimmer came in and said, 'You'll bonk anything won't you, Lister?' It was a very funny moment, and took my attention away from the snake section, for which, in rehearsal, I used an old scarf.

Off we go to Manchester, on the coach, tra la la. The next day is a long and gruelling time in the studio, shooting all the polymorph changes, the rabbit which wouldn't hop, the ball which wouldn't roll, the shami kebab which wouldn't wriggle. In the end they all did. The following day we start camera rehearsals and when we get to the snake part, Donna walks in with a stuffed tube of cotton painted to look a bit like a snake. It was probably about twelve feet long. I assumed this was meant to represent the snake. I laughed. I was getting used to these guys, always joshing about. We rehearsed with this great long sausage until it was time for me to complete my make-up.

On camera-rehearsal days in Manchester, I used to have the unpainted mask stuck on during the day, and have it finished off between the end of rehearsals and when the audience arrived. As soon as my make-up was finished, Donna took me along the corridor into a small room. I was wearing only a pair of underpants because I get so hot in the mask it's the only way to stay coolish. In the room was a woman and a large picnic hamper. She opened the lid and I was introduced to Tina. Tina was a sixteen-foot long, seven-stone python. She grinned at me, as if to say, You don't half look a prat, with that mask on and virtually nothing else.

The woman who owned Tina picked her out of the basket. Tina was a snake, i.e., she was supposed to be long and thin. She was long, but her middle section was thicker than my thigh, and she was heavy. They drooped her over my shoulder. It was like giving a shoulder ride to a fourteen-year-old kid. A big fourteen-year-old kid.

I have to say Tina was great to work with, very professional. I felt calm and relaxed. As I handed her back to the owner, I noticed double puncture marks all up the woman's forearm. I asked about these strange-looking marks. 'Oh, she will bite, but it's not poisonous. It does hurt a bit, and you need an anti-tetanus jab, but she's not dangerous.' There we go, the old irony warning light has been on all this time and I didn't even notice.

Once we were in the studio and it came to Tina's entrance, the show was kicking, as Danny would say. As the owner slowly pulled Tina out of her basket, the audience screamed. People squirmed in their seats as they watched this massive snake uncoil from her basket. She was hooked over my shoulders and I had to hold her head up, look at her face and say 'Snake!'

That's all, it was a very brief shot. That's comedy. In the event Tina didn't bite me, although she wouldn't do exactly as Ed wanted. When I tried to lift her head up, I felt her enormous strength as she suggested to me that she didn't want her head lifted up. She could easily have squeezed around my neck hard enough to pop my head off my shoulders.

Here's the irony. If you watch a tape of this episode, you'd have to use freeze-frame to see even a shot of me and Tina struggling to the death. However, the next moment has gone down in *Red Dwarf* history as one of the best moments. Craig and the shrinking boxer shorts.

OK, so I have toured the world (he said grandly) making people laugh. I have succeeded and failed. I have had them rolling in the aisles. I have had to delay my next line to accommodate the laugh. I've done shows where I know the laugh is coming and I've milked it. But never, in all those thousands of performances, have I ever experienced a moment like this.

My ear was no more than four feet from Craig's mouth. He was screaming his lines out to me, I was screaming mine back at him. Neither of us could hear a thing. The audience made such a noise that we couldn't hear ourselves think. Chris had to wait for ages and ages to say his you'll-bonk-anything-Lister line. He just stood there looking at us with that face of his. That was enough for the live audience, they went bananas.

The coach ride home that night was electric. Danny was re-enacting the show scene by scene for all of us, which was odd considering we'd all been there.

'They were laughing so much, man, Robby couldn't hear his cue, man. We are talking a major woof, man. I mean, that was a prime-quality woof, you know what I'm saying?' Someone else would try and say something, but Danny was still in full flow. 'Shrinkin' boxer shorts, man. A classic woof, I'm tellin' you, that'll go down in history, guy.'

By the time of the third episode rehearsals I had got into my stride. I had started to remember everyone's name: John Pomphrey, the lighting man; Rocket, the head cameraman; Ron Tufnell, one of the cameramen who had also worked on *The Corner-house* with me; Mel Bibby, the man who designed the sets and props; Keith Mayes, the sound man; Howard Burden, the costume man.

During the technical run-through all these people and more would be standing around going through their scripts as we went through the episode. Ed Bye would stand where the camera was going to be and point at whoever was in the shot. This was a great help to us as we would then know where the camera we were playing to was going to be.

I was getting used to the lunches in the BBC canteen, I was less impressed when I saw a famous person, I was getting blasé. One day, when Stephen Fry and Hugh Laurie and all the *Blackadder* people were involved in a big benefit concert called The Pretty Policeman's Ball, Ed Asner, the actor who portrayed Lou Grant in the series of the same name, walked past me. I was impressed with him because he was old and American and a proper actor. Jerry Hall walked past me next; I was impressed with her because she's famous and knows Mick Jagger biblically. Someone else walked past me who I didn't know and I was still impressed because I am very bad at recognizing famous people so it could have been anyone.

The one episode in series three when I had a lot of mates in the cast was *Backwards*. Tony Hawks and Arthur Smith were both old troopers from the comedy circuit. Well, not that old, about the same age as me. Arthur and I had done one of the most unpleasant gigs of our careers together, in a dungeon down a narrow alley in Edinburgh. It was during the Festival, in 1987 I think, and we had both been talked into doing a spot at a youth club. I was trying out material for a new stand-up set, and I'm a cheap show-off, so I was happy to do it. Arthur had a new suit and wanted to try that out. The youth club was very rough, most of the youth were in their twenties, very drunk, and looked like the sort of people a crusty would avoid.

There was a stage and on the stage were four students doing some sort of weird piece of theatre. They were being showered by beer mats and spit, but I didn't panic. I'm a professional. I was wearing a suit and tie, and the piece involved me doing a striptease down to a super-revealing Lycra body suit, which, if I hit it right, could theoretically be very funny.

I went up on to the stage and the booing and hissing was very loud, the beer mats started to fly, and then a beer glass. I took hold of the mike stand and shouted, 'Thank you very much, and good-night.' It was the shortest show I have ever done. I fled the place before Arthur went on.

About two hours later I turned up at the Assembly Rooms bar and saw Arthur standing in another suit, holding a plastic carrier bag. I asked him what had happened.

'I was doing quite well, all things considered, they'd stopped throwing glasses and bottles, and I was beginning to get a few laughs, then a bloke walked up to me and poured a pint of piss over my head.'

It became a favourite anecdote of the Festival. That's why I say old trooper, or maybe it should be nutter. How many of us would continue in a line of work after being abused like that by a customer?

Backwards, in which Arthur played the barman, became an immensely complicated episode. The script had worked out all the difficult areas of reverse logic. The only bit which confused us all was the fight sequence, where we had to work out when Craig's injuries disappeared, and how he would feel slowly worse until he reached the fight, when the pain would be unpunched out of him. This episode has gone down in *Red Dwarf* history as being one of the best, but when we were making it, it became harder and harder to understand what was going on.

My biggest problem all the way through series three was trying to learn my lines. At home I had started to wear a groove in the kitchen floor, pacing up and down for hours as I tried to get these complicated lines into my head. Rob and Doug's language is so unique and so free of cliché that a long Kryten speech is very hard to learn.

When I have learned other people's scripts, I have found that there is usually a turn of phrase or a sentence structure that you recognize and you already have at your disposal. It's therefore fairly easy to learn as you almost know it already, you only have to memorize it in order.

With Kryten talk, this is never the case. Rob and Doug will never use a hackneyed turn of phrase, they always come up with new ways of saying something. This is one reason I love their scripts when I first read them, and hate their guts as I try and learn them.

There were times as the third series wore on where a new Kryten line would make us all laugh simply because it was so tortuous. The standing joke was that Rob and Doug would write me a five-page explanatory speech, telling the rest of the crew how black holes work, or that time dilation would save us from the horrific fate overhanging us. This speech would be very long and very hard to learn, and it would usually start with the word 'Listen . . .' At the end, Danny would smile, show his teeth and say, 'I was with you until you said listen.' This would of course bring the house down.

In the rehearsal room were two old bunk-beds* that stood in for the beds in the officers' quarters where a lot of the action in series three took place. On most mornings, I would arrive, script in hand, still trying to do that killer speech on page seven. Donna DiStefano would be going through her props, Ed Bye would be pacing around working out his camera script. Chris Barrie would be on his mobile phone trying to fend off offers of work and see if he could fit in a four o'clock. It took me a while to find out what a four o'clock was. I know that during the war the gunners in British and American bombers used to point out enemy fighters to each other using the clock as a common reference: 'The Hun at five o'clock high, chaps, give 'em hell.' However, Chris Barrie's four o'clock is a voice-over recording at four o'clock in the afternoon, with luck after rehearsals. Not quite so brave and dashing as the World War II gunners reference, but with a charm all of its own.

On the top bunk there would be an inanimate lump, otherwise known as a sleeping Craig Charles;

* Under one of these beds was written in felt-tip pen, NORMAN LOVETT WAS HERE FOR QUITE A WHILE.

in the lower bunk would be a far more elegant body, stretched out but, likewise, fast asleep. This would be the graceful frame of Danny John Jules.

Everyone would work quietly, so as not to wake them until rehearsals began at ten o'clock. I have no idea what Danny and Craig did during the night in those days, but it clearly didn't involve sleep. They made me feel so old. They did in fact call me grand-dad for a while when we each revealed our ages over lunch. Well, Hattie wouldn't reveal hers, I politely didn't ask, being a nice, middle-class, well-brought-up boy. However, such niceties didn't hold Craig back, who immediately said, 'Come on, Hat, how old are you, man?' Hattie wasn't having it, and her age remains a mystery to all of us to this day.

When they found out how old I was, they were amazed. 'I'll be dead before I'm that age, man,' said Craig. 'I've peaked already, man, I'm twenty-four and I'm burnt out.' When I gave him a lift home that night he was quite animated. Normally Craig fell asleep as soon as he closed the car door, but this time there was no stopping him. 'It's amazing how old you are and you're still going. I'm shagged, man,' he said. 'I started in this game when I was sixteen, doin' poetry and that. I got married real young, I was on telly regularly by the time I was eighteen. I've got there too quick, man, now I'm shagged out, I'm burnt out, man, there's nothing left, I'm a husk. It's all over for me, man. I'll never get to your age.'

I was very worried for Craig. I have a weakness

when I listen to other people: I always believe what I'm told. The next day I had foolishly expected Craig to be likewise subdued, but he was bouncing about like a spring chicken. Looking back on his speech now, from five years later, it does seem rather amusing.

Craig has immense energy, and an annoyingly good memory. I say annoying for two reasons. One is that he can pick up the script, look at it a couple of times and then lose it, and he knows all his lines, knows all Danny's lines and knows most of mine. The other thing is that he has a good memory for conversations and statements. I could say something one year, and then contradict it the next, as I am wont to do, and the only person who remembers what I said before is Craig.

'That's not what you said last year,' he'll say with a cheeky grin.

'Isn't it?' I'll say, racking my brains trying to remember what I might have said.

'No, on January the twenty-third, you said completely the opposite.' The annoying thing is he'll be right.

I have learned though that remembering lines is very much to do with trust. In the episode titled *Timeslides*, the one where Kryten got to do a bit of air guitar work in the darkroom, I had to do a difficult speech, apologizing to Rimmer for referring to his mother as an old trout. 'I compared your mother to an aged blubbery fish . . .' and on and on.

Try as I might that week, this speech got the better of me. Hattie tried to help me remember it by breaking the speech into a list of first letters. That meant '. . . an aged blubbery fish, a simple-minded scaly old piscine . . .' became ABFASMSOP.

It was hopeless. I couldn't remember a word of it. Nothing seemed to help. I was very downhearted about it and constantly lost my temper when trying to memorize it. If I stumbled in rehearsals I would bark out, 'Don't tell me, I know it, I know it!' and then promptly prove that I didn't know anything.

On the night of the recording, Mike Agnew, the super-hardworking production manager who falls asleep in the back of the bus, had provided an idiot board with the speech written in capital letters. He tucked it away behind part of the set so the audience wouldn't see it before the scene, the idea being that he would turn it round just before saying action.

Under the pressure of the moment, no one remembered to turn the card round before we started recording the scene. As there are always nine hundred things going on at once, it was hardly surprising. The first few exchanges between Kryten and Rimmer went very well. Chris had huge long speeches to do, twice, three times as much as me, and he sailed through them beautifully. As we approached my killer speech, I noticed out of the corner of my eye Mike Agnew crawling across the floor, desperately trying to reach my cue card. I realized what was going on but somehow didn't panic and started the

Simon Fanshaw pictured in the
crush of the Assembly Rooms
Bar. 'Darling, you haven't won
the Perrier!'

Arthur Smith showing that he is a
well-balanced individual with a
good dentist.

The play that started it all for me. *Mammon, Robot Born of Woman*.
The woman in question is the wonderful Deb'bora John Wilson.

In the heady innocent days before I even knew what a full-face prosthetic rubber piece was. You can't see the shoes very well but they were hand-embroidered green-and-red hippie slippers.

Sitting in my workshop next to the Thames in Bermondsey. The boots were for a woman who danced at the Raymond Revuebar in Soho.

We're The J-O-E-Y Joeys. Me, Chris Eymard, Bernie Evans and
Nigel Ordish. (Photo credit: Frank Ainsworth)

The cast of *Onan*, the play I did during the recording of series 3. The
man with the precarious glasses is John McKay.
(Photo credit: Steve Double)

The engagement photo. Kryten and Camille. Aaaah.

Kryten gets to see himself on telly. 'Hmm, so much fuss over such crude technology.'

End of series 6, and Craig Charles snips off his locks. Takes him all year to grow and thirty seconds to loose. At this point Craig is saying, 'Oh man, what a f****** relief!'

Yes indeed, sir. Mr Chris Barrie looking bright, bushy-tailed and most certainly on the ball. UUuuuu, extraordinary.

What's happenin', guy! Mr Danny John Jules getting ready to kick some comedy booty.

Hattie Hayridge standing on the set with a chain growing out of her head. Photography not being my strong point.

Me on a beach in Australia, on my way to Hollywood, practising the word 'rich'. Five weeks later I was sitting in a North London kitchen reminding myself of the words 'get real, airhead'.

Well, you have to do this in Australia at least once. And yes, he did kack all over my shirt.

(*Above*) The comedy police hit the floor. Doug Naylor follows Rob Grant on to the set. 'Bit of a rewrite, guys, big new speech for you, Bobby, quite technical actually and only three minutes to learn it. Ha ha ha.'

(*Left*) Peter Wragg, my hero, at the last night party for series 5.

Sitting in my own chair in Hollywood, with a cup of water which I could drink, talking to Elizabeth Moorhead who played Kochanski. Ahh, stardom, power, glory... and a return ticket.

speech with ease. I managed to get through it, not word-perfect, but close enough. It was the first time I'd ever got past the first phrase. Meanwhile Mike was in an agonizing position by my feet, and I had to step over him in order to do my exit.

It's amazing what an audience can do for a performer when the pressure is on. The more hours I'd spent trying to learn this speech, the less I could remember; the more angry I got, the more hopeless it became. As soon as I relaxed, it was fine.

I've often wondered if proper actors have been taught how to learn lines. By proper actors, I mean the ones who went to drama school. I didn't go to drama school. In fact, I barely went to school at all. I was forever running away and skiving off to smoke cigarettes and practise swearing.

I did though try to go to drama school once, after I'd been performing for a bit. I thought I'd give it a go. I knew I could get a grant because I'd never been to university.

I applied to get into the Central School of Speech and Drama, in St John's Wood, London. I got a form and an explanatory booklet. I had to learn two bits of Shakespeare and one bit of contemporary. I borrowed *The Complete Works of Shakespeare* from a friend and found the passages. Bit of *Hamlet*, bit of *Two Gentlemen of Verona*. Neither of them made any sense to me at all, although I'd seen both plays and enjoyed them. I asked another friend what contemporary bit of theatre to do. I fancied something like a speech from the film *Bullitt* starring Steve McQueen. I was told this wasn't quite appropriate, and in the end we settled on a speech from *The Threepenny Opera* by Bertolt Brecht.

I spent a couple of evenings trying to learn this stuff, then turned up at the school for my interview. I sat in a room full of men who looked just like me. My height, my hair colour, my build. The only difference was they were all quite good at acting. I was eventually shown into a room where three people sat behind a table. They asked me to do my Shakespeare, I nodded calmly, stood up, and shook my hands about in an actory sort of way. The three people looked expectant. I stood like a Shakespearian character and said ... nothing. I couldn't remember a thing.

'Would you like a prompt?' someone asked. I had no idea what a prompt was, but I nodded seriously.

'"What kind of man is this?"' said a man who was sitting behind me.

'Oh yeah, that's it,' I said. 'I remember now, "What kind of man is this" ... um ... don't tell me, I'll get it in a bit.'

Hopeless. They didn't ask to see my other Shakespeare, but asked for a bit of the contemporary piece. They asked what I was going to do. I couldn't remember what it was called.

'It's a sort of musical by this German bloke. It's got songs in it, really famous songs.'

'Kurt Weill?' said one of the people behind the table, helpfully.

'Could have been,' I said, scratching my head.

'Bertolt Brecht?' said another.

'That's the fellow,' I said, pointing at them and clicking my fingers. 'It's a piece by Bertolt Brecht called Mack something.'

' "Mack the Knife?" '

'You know it, don't you?' I said, smiling.

'Yes,' said the man behind the table, 'but I don't think you do.'

'Come and sit down and tell us a bit about yourself, Robert,' said the woman who was sitting next to him. 'Why do you want to become an actor?'

'Oh, I don't really want to be an actor, I'm just a show-off really, but I can get a grant for three years, you see, so I thought I wouldn't have to work.'

The three people behind the table nodded gravely, but they didn't give up.

'Have you had any acting experience?'

'Not really, not proper acting, I've done a lot of comedy and mime stuff. Street entertaining and cabaret.'

'Have you done any fencing?'

I thought this was a bit of an odd question, I thought they were talking about acting and suddenly he asks about fencing. The thing was, I had done fencing.

'Well, yes,' I said, 'I did quite a lot of fencing on a farm I used to work on. Mostly wire mesh but some post-and-rail stuff.'

I was thanked for my time and told to ask the next

young hopeful to come in as I left. I thought I'd done pretty well, all things considered. They didn't offer me a place, strangely enough.

I have since discovered that proper actors don't get lessons in how to remember lines. They just get a lot of practice, and like most things, the more you do it, the easier it becomes.

The last episode of series three (*The Last Day*) was a favourite of mine because for one fairly large section I wore an evening suit, which was far more comfortable than the normal Kryten uniform. Also, because it was the last episode of the series, there was a bit of a party atmosphere going around, and indeed there was to be a party after the show.

As the make-up came off for the last time, I breathed a huge sigh of relief. Never again would I have to sit still for five hours having someone dab my face with a sponge. Never again would my eyes be glued open and have bright lights shone in them. Never again would I sweat so much each day I wouldn't have to take a pee. It was all over. For ever.

As I walked from the BBC studios to the rooms where we were having the last-night party, I was a deeply happy individual. I felt a great sense of achievement. I'd worn a full-face, full-head prosthetic mask for eighteen days, and I hadn't killed myself or anyone else.

The party was great fun. I'd made friends with a lot of new people but I knew what would happen: as soon as we all went our separate ways, no matter what promises we'd make, we'd never see each other again.

At one point Chris Barrie stood up in the corner of the room and did a short routine depicting a day on the *Red Dwarf* set which had everyone on the floor laughing. His impressions of Rob, Doug and Ed were amazing in their accuracy. His Craig Charles was breathtaking: 'Hey, man, I do me own stunts, just stuff a load of explosives down me jockstrap, no problem, man.' He did a wonderfully funny impression of Peter Wragg, the special effects and model wizard, and his Danny John Jules was magnificent. Watching the faces of the people who were being impersonated was fascinating. They stared with slack jaw, trying to work out who it was he was doing. People very rarely recognize themselves, but everyone else does immediately. Chris only had to pull a face and we all knew who he was being. He didn't do a Robert Llewellyn at the party; I would have to wait for that dubious privilege.

The next morning it was the long and, even for me, slightly hung-over coach ride back to Acton. Once in the car park we bid our farewells and that was an end to it. I had great fun doing the series, but they had made three and the general feeling going around was that this was the last one.

CHAPTER 5

I didn't see the warning light, I didn't hear the Klaxon. In the huge irony control room in the sky, men in white coats were running about with clipboards, making notes. 'Looks like 8289–27663–RL is going through an irony warp,' says an operative who starts punching in data. I didn't hear them, I didn't know that 8289–27663–RL was me.

On 5 November 1990, less than a year since I had the last mask removed, I was sitting in a make-up chair in a location make-up lorry, parked next to a huge disused pumping station just below a flyover in West London. I was having a new mask stuck on.

When I say a new mask I mean this was a completely new mask. Many people don't realize that each time Kryten appears on the screen, it's actually a new mask. I can only wear them once, they're like paper knickers, wear once and throw them away. When they're removed, they're ripped to bits, quite often by me, so that my make-up chair is surrounded by sweaty bits of Kryten's head. Sad really.

In the intervening year I'd been to see a skin

---

* I'd done many other exciting, entertaining and educational things as well. I didn't sit at home all year and then go to a skin allergist for an afternoon. I just wanted to make that clear.

allergist,* and found out that I am allergic to nothing except exhaustion. The reason my face was so sore the year before was because it had a rubber mask stuck all over it all day. 'What d'you expect?' said the doctor.

I had been to have my head recast. I went back to the BBC special effects department in Acton, where I met Andrea Pennel. She was the new head make-up person on *Red Dwarf IV*. She watched as they made another mould of my head and then she and Peter Wragg pointed at the cast with pens and rulers and measuring tapes. They tapped it, drew lines on it, and talked for ages about feather-edges and splits, about foam compounds and cooking times. I nodded in my special I-understand-all-about-foam type of way, when in reality I was thinking about kinky sex.

For the fourth series I had two new make-up women, Andrea and Fiona Kemp. I say they were my make-up women, of course they weren't, they were independent women who controlled their own destiny. Not only that, they also did Chris and Craig's make-up, so there was very little exclusivity about the arrangement. They did spend more time with me though, and it is a well-known fact in the entertainment industry that make-up women know everything about their artists and everything about the production company and everything about everything really. Quite a lot of male performers marry their make-up women, but I'd just like to state now, unequivocally, that I have never had sexual congress with a make-up woman.

After a few long sessions, even the tongue of a seasoned non-gossiper starts to wiggle a bit. As for me, I am blurting everything out before my arse hits the chair. I walk in the door in the morning and before they can say, 'Good morning, Robert,' I'm off.

'I'm really depressed about my life, I feel old and fat, I don't think my girlfriend fancies me anymore, I don't think my mum ever really loved me, I'm very confused about my life and sexuality, I don't know what to do about my career, I quite fancy the woman who's doing the vision-mixing, what d'you know about her? No I shouldn't. I'm in a regular, on-going-type relationship which I'm really happy in, at least I think I'm happy . . .' This is before I take my coat off.

'Are you warm enough, Robert?' asked Andrea on that first morning in the make-up truck. Andrea always goes for the simple solution to solve problems first. If you're cold, she gets the fire on. If you're depressed about the state of the universe, she needs a couple of hours to sort it out.

Fiona was a very patient woman too. She had a small baby boy who she had to leave at the crack of dawn to stand by my rubber head and sniff glue for three or four hours a day. Fiona did have a tendency to lose glue brushes though. The glue they use to attach Kryten's head to me is some sort of medical, heavy-duty skin-ripper stuff, which dries very quickly and was used in Vietnam for sticking GIs stomachs together to 'Get them heli-vacced the hell outa here!'

Kaboom, rat-at-at-tat. 'I love the smell of napalm, it's the smell of victory . . .'

Fiona would stand by me for minutes at a time looking all over the place for the missing glue brush which was invariably stuck to my back or the arm of the chair or something.

It was very early in the morning that first day, and bitterly cold. Everyone on the crew was wearing those big quilted jackets that film-crew-type people always wear on location. I was boiling. Once you cover every inch of your head in rubber, you're warm, full stop.

Chris, Craig and Danny were all standing around shivering. I think this was one of the two or three times in four years when I almost felt more sorry for them than I did for myself.

'Ahh, perfect weather for Kryten,' I said as I joined them.

'Shut up, you smug bastard,' said Craig, then laughed through his teeth and hustled someone for a cigarette.

Craig and cigarettes. OK, it's a little-known fact that Craig Charles is on a mission, which is to borrow a cigarette off every living smoker on the planet. He has so far clocked up 47,815 people. This isn't to say Craig never buys them. He buys them and loses them. In fact, during the read-through of the fourth series, he came in with hundreds of packs of cigarettes and distributed them around the room.

Even here, in this obscure corner of irony control,

there was a little light flashing. In January 1990 I gave up smoking. I'd been a smoker for nearly twenty years. Ever since I had a pull on a number six filter tip behind the chemistry lab,★ I was hooked. This time, however, I'd really kicked the habit. I have a very strange photograph someone took during the making of the third series where you can see Kryten smoking. It looks all wrong somehow. Kryten wouldn't understand smoking, and it would make laundry smell, which is such a shame.

We were standing around in the cold because we were once again filming inserts for the next series. Once I was fully kitted up in Kryten's Krippling Kostume I climbed the wide stairs, carefully not tripping over the thick twists of cable that ran from the generator trucks to the array of lights John Pomphrey had installed.

The inside of the building was a breathtaking sight: two gigantic steam-driven pumps, one at either end of the building. A giant Meccano set of a machine which once upon a time pumped water up to thirty miles away, feeding millions of homes and businesses. It has long since been shut down, but I had the strange feeling I'd seen it before. As I wandered around the vast echoing chamber I asked John Pomphrey why it might be that I recognized it.

'*Chitty Chitty Bang Bang* was filmed here,' said

★ The bike sheds were in full view of the headmaster's office in my school.

John, as though everyone had been asking him all day. They had.

'Toot sweet,' I said. 'The Toot sweet song, of course.'

I wandered about the building singing 'Toot sweet, toot sweet, the pom poms you blow on, the whistles you eat,' dressed as a mechanoid with a rubber head. Irony warning light number seven blew a fuse. I was beginning to understand how to get through this time. It helped me if I went slightly mad. I seemed to end up in the oddest places with a rubber head on. It was best, I felt, if I sang a song from a popular children's film of the sixties. Preferably featuring the many talents of Mister Dick Van Dyke.

We spent the rest of the day wearing ridiculous foam-rubber-and-plastic flashing shoes called escort boots. These were made at great expense and with great difficulty by the Peter Wragg Diva Posse, as they'd come to be known. We broke them within about ten minutes, the combination of our clumsiness and the fact that, as a cast, we are very good at breaking props. We can break virtually anything. However, we had great fun stomping about in these things that were almost impossible to walk in. They escorted us into the justice zone, another of Rob and Doug's brilliant concepts: a zone where whatever crime you commit, the resultant misfortune happens to you. I mean, how do they come up with it? What goes through their minds? When we're actually *in situ*, working out how to film something, it rarely occurs to me where all these ideas come from. I suppose they must sit around and say things like:

'What would happen if you were in a world where crime was impossible?'

'How could it be impossible?'

'If every time you committed a crime it was against yourself.'

'Yeah, no, yeah. Good. So there'd be no point to crime so you'd stop.'

'You'd never start.'

'Yeah, no, yeah, you'd never start, and if you gave someone a present, you'd get it back.'

'Yeah. Great. And if you whacked them over the head with a hammer, you'd feel the pain yourself.'

That's how those two men earn their living, by coming up with absurd notions and developing them into story lines.

Of course when I'm trying to learn some difficult lines late at night, wearing a mini Grand Canyon into my kitchen floor, I can imagine another bit of their conversation.

'OK, we've got our story lines worked out, the structure's there, right? OK, what we really need to do now is –'

'Give Robert some really hard speeches to learn!'

'Yeah, yeah, ha ha ha.'

'Ha ha ha.'

'I compared your mother to a bloated blubbery fish.'

'A simple-minded scaly old piscine.'

'Ah ha ha. That really screwed him in the last series didn't it? Soft middle-class bastard.'

'Did you see his face as he was trying to learn that? Hopeless. He spent hours trying to do that one.'

'Hey, hey. Hold on, steady. Hold on. Here we go, what about, in *Justice*, when Rimmer is on trial for killing the crew of *Red Dwarf*, Kryten has to defend him.'

'And do a very long speech.'

'A very very long speech. Yeah. With lots of facts and twisted logic in it.'

'Yeah, yeah. Fantastic. A long speech. Ten, twelve pages.'

'Yeah, that'll do his head in. Know-all bastard.'

'Smug git.'

'Hey, hey, I know what will really do him in!'

'What, what, what?'

'Right at the very end, right, at the very very end, when he's done this long, killer speech, we give Danny a one-word punch-line and a massive woof!'

'Yeah, yeah, no, yeah. Great.'

I'm sure nothing of the sort really happens. None of us in the cast will ever know what they say about us, but sometimes we think we can guess, just by what happens to us in the series. Craig gets blown up, strangled, shot to bits and covered in curry. He says:

'Hey, guys, how come I'm always the one that gets done in? What have I done?'

'You got up this morning,' says Rob as he walks past.

'They're hard bastards,' says Craig.

'Very bitter men,' I say.

'Very bitter hard bastards,' says Chris, 'who happen to be very deeply talented.'

'I ain't saying nothin', geezer,' says Danny.

Teasing Rob and Doug is one of the mainstays of our weekly routine when we are recording a series. They are referred to as the boys, the comedy Gestapo, the comedy boot boys, the comedy police and keep your heads down, they're in.

They take this ribbing very well, in the spirit in which it is intended. 'Shut your face, you bastard,' says Rob as he head-butts you. No, no, I jest. It's all good, clean boysy fun. They are very involved in the day-to-day process of creating the series, and by series four the production company had changed from Paul Jackson Productions to Grant Naylor Productions.

'Hey, Rob and Doug, la,'* says Craig during a read-through session, 'got your own production company now I see. Grant Naylor, you'll have a helicopter next, la.'

'It's on order,' says Doug.

'But when we get it,' says Rob, 'you can't have a ride in it.'

---

* For some reason, which is still a mystery to the rest of the cast and crew, Craig Charles peppered his speech with the word la during series four. He didn't use this term in series three or series five, by which time the rest of us were walking around saying things like, What's going on, la? and D'you want a cup of tea, la? Obviously by then, saying la had become *passé*.

Rob Grant's nickname is Doctor Love. He's the man everyone turns to with their problems. I've had dreams where Rob is on a radio phone-in programme, with people ringing him up to get advice.

'Doctor Love, what do I do, my wife's left me?' asks a distraught caller.

'It's your own fault, you miserable bastard,' answers Doctor Love.

Series four was a very different experience for everyone though. The first three series had been rehearsed in London and recorded in Manchester. This time we were under a completely new regime. We rehearsed and recorded in the same studio, G Stage at Shepperton. Officially this was decided because the shooting was so technical and it would be easier for all concerned if we had access to the set all week. I think the real reason was to give everyone a hard time by forcing them to go to Shepperton every day.

Shepperton is the flat bit with the reservoirs you fly over as you come in to land at Heathrow Airport. If you've never flown in to Heathrow Airport, that won't help you, so let's just say it's on the western fringe of London, just inside the M25, quite near the Thames. The studios have a wonderful feel to them. It's easy to imagine them being a hive of activity in the fifties, when all those war movies and *Carry On* films were made there. The studio lot is actually in the garden of a posh old house, the interior of which we used to record part of the *Meltdown* episode.

What now takes place in the eight or nine cavernous studios is mostly TV commercials with the occasional series like *Red Dwarf* and *Alias Smith and Jones*. Basically it's seen better days.

When we were there the first year, we kept seeing all these long-haired men with dirty cloaks wandering about. It was like being at Glastonbury Fayre all over again, great hordes of wandering hippies stumbling about. Sometimes in the Shepperton canteen you'd find yourself standing in the queue behind forty heavily armed medieval soldiers. After a while we found out they were involved in a film, *Robin Hood, Prince of Thieves*, which starred Kevin Costner.

Yes, I did see Kev. Well, OK, I didn't actually see him, but I was walking along the road in Shepperton and this huge stretch limo rumbled past. It had tinted windows so there was no way of knowing who was in there, but I could feel Kev's presence. Mike McShane was playing Friar Tuck. I met him one day in the car park and he showed me the set. Up behind one of the studios was an enormous castle, made of polystyrene and paint, scaffold and chipboard. It looked completely real, with a huge castle yard full of old peasants and weird farm animals, cows with big horns, odd-looking sheep and pigs. It was a lot more exciting than being in the studio.

Being at Shepperton meant we spent the best part of seven weeks shut up in the huge studio, sitting in the set, living in the set and, in Craig's case, occasionally sleeping in the set.

Before we started recording Ed Bye had asked me if I had any suggestions for a woman to play the part of Camille, the female mechanoid that Kryten had to fall in love with. I pondered how cheap it would be to suggest Judy Pascoe, my real-life girlfriend of four years. I struggled with this dilemma for three quarters of a second, then said, 'There's this actress called Judy Pascoe I know vaguely, you could try her, she is Australian, but she can do a very good mid-Atlantic accent.'

They saw Judy and liked her. She got the job, so after all the moaning and complaining she'd had to listen to from me the year before, she was going to try a mask on herself. She was going to know what it was like to go under rubber.

It wasn't, as I feared it might be, a problem working with Judy on an episode of *Red Dwarf*. She knew Craig from a few years before. He'd made a programme called *Craig Goes Mad in Melbourne* about the Melbourne Comedy Festival in Australia. Judy had won the Melbourne Comedy Festival prize that year for her show *The Last Great Adventure*, and Craig had interviewed her on the programme.

I think problems with couples who work together stem from some form of competitiveness between them, and thankfully we didn't suffer from that. I mean, sure, Judy was very popular with the cast and crew. They all really really liked her and thought she was funny and patient, and a really nice person. They still ask about her to this day, not that I'm bitter. So what, if she only did one episode and people still remember her three or four years later. That's fine, that's what being in love is all about. Bitch.

On the pre-record day Judy and I both had to turn up extra early to get made-up. As there were now two masks to apply, Fiona and Andrea had their work cut out. They got me done first because I was 'hardened to it'. Fair enough.

I was in the studio when I first saw Judy in full make-up. It was a very strange experience, seeing someone you know so well disappear behind rubber. You look at them and you can't recognize them at all, your eye searches madly for some sign. I first saw the back of her head and I didn't want her to turn round. I didn't know what it was going to be like to see her face. It's the eyes, that's all you have left. I could just about recognize her eyes.

When Judy had come up to Manchester the year before to watch us record the last episode, she had been very shocked when she first saw me in the mask. She didn't want to look, and when I tried to give her a kiss on the cheek, she screamed. I don't want to give the impression that Judy is some sort of wimp: she spent five years touring the world in a circus company, climbing up poles and balancing three eggs on a chopstick on her nose. I suppose, however, circus work doesn't prepare you for seeing your boyfriend with someone else's face on. Being a stand-up comic and show-off doesn't prepare you for seeing the woman you love with a square bald head either.

However, it was quite romantic reliving our real-life meeting when encased in rubber and plastic. Judy and I did experience an advanced mutual compatibility on the basis of a primary initial ident, or, in human terms, love at first sight, so we related to the story on that level.

During the pre-record day, when no one was looking, around the back of the set, Kryten and Camille attempted to kiss. It wasn't like kissing through glass, or even kissing through two very thin layers of prosthetic rubber. It was like kissing with a local anaesthetic, through a thick army blanket.

The picture of Kryten and Camille together has become our favourite. My mum and dad have a framed print up on their wall. When my mum shows guests her family snapshots, she says, 'This is my eldest son with his wife and children, this is my daughter and her children, and this is my middle son who's a robot, and that's his girlfriend.'

During the recording of *Camille*, I had to hang from a gantry, held up by straps around my lower gentleman's parts. Peter Wragg had set it up. 'It's like a parachute harness, Robert, don't worry, it's very safe,' he said. 'Just make sure you're comfortable before you put your weight on it.'

What he meant by comfortable was if you didn't get all your bits in the right place it could really catch your breath as you swung free. It felt fine when I was standing on my feet, but as soon as I swung out, I realized I was doing irreparable damage to the family jewels.

I was meant to be hanging from this gantry, being filmed from below, with no way out: Kryten was doomed. Then came the moment where Camille saves Kryten's life. As I was hanging and they were setting up the camera to try and find the shot, I was busy complaining away as usual. 'Ooh, the straps are killing me, I can't breathe. Oh God, I'm in agony.'

You would think that you might get a bit of sympathy from your partner in a situation like this. You might hope she would reach out to you and say, 'Oh, you are brave, my warrior, you are so tough and manly.'

However, now my partner was covered in rubber and as uncomfortable as me, there was no chance.

'Oh, stop complaining, y' dag,' she called from above.

'That's right, Jude, you tell him,' said Craig.

'And you can shut up, Craig, you're a double dag, mate,' she snapped breezily. For those not familiar with Australian parlance, a dag is the lump of fly-infested sheep excrement which dangles from the wool around a sheep's rear downstairs section. Craig seemed quite pleased with the term.

Camille was great fun to do though, especially dancing with a four-foot-high green blob with an eye on a stalk who talked like my girlfriend.

During the week we were recording *White Hole*, Ed Bye was preoccupied with the imminent arrival of his second child, prepared to leave at a moment's notice to be with his wife Ruby for the delivery.

As the laws of irony would have it, the morning Ed didn't turn up was the morning of the actual recording. By the time the cast arrived, the whole day had been hurriedly arranged by fax, phone and courier bike. Paul Jackson, the original producer of the show, and by this time a very successful TV executive, was roped in at the last moment. Paul has a reputation in the business for being a man who gets the job done. He doesn't like to hang around and work out the philosophy behind the joke.

'Paul, I er, don't really know what this line is about,' says the concerned actor.

'Bugger what it's about, do the line, get the laugh, and we can all get off home,' says Paul Jackson. Well, who knows really but this is a quote which is often attributed to him.

Paul arrived just after I got to the studio. He said he was nervous but very pleased to be doing it. The atmosphere in the studio was electric; for some reason the crew were more on their toes than usual. I don't wish to give the impression that they are a lazy bunch of slobs: they all work very hard to get the show done on time. But the day Paul Jackson walked on to the floor, you had to watch those guys to believe it.

As we went through the camera rehearsal, what normally might have been a technical problem of some difficulty would be solved in an instant. It seemed to us that men were walking around prepared to die in order to get the shot. We saw men knocking nails into the set with their bare hands, men pulling nails out of the set with their teeth. There was no stopping them.

However, one person who didn't quite give Paul the support he was looking for was Danny. This was the only day I can remember Danny being late on a studio day. He walked in and of course got teased to death by Craig.

'Your balls are on the line, la,' he said as Danny breezed in.

'I got held up, guy,' said Danny.

'Dan, the big Jacko is in, Ed's with Ruby, havin' the baby, la, and you're late, la.'

'Jacko is in today?' said Danny, incredulously.

'Yes, but it'll all be fine,' I said, trying to make Dan calm down. 'You're all right, Dan, he really likes you.'

At that point Paul walked on to the set.

'Oh, Danny, you're here, that's nice of you,' he said. 'It's nice to know I can rely on my friends when I'm in big trouble. Good of you to drop by, hope we're not keeping you from anything.'

Danny stood frozen to the spot, a big smile plastered across his face. Paul whispered something in his ear. Danny never would tell me what he said. Danny looked mortified for a moment, then laughed very loudly. Paul clapped his hands. 'OK, let's get on and then we can all go for lunch.'

Considering Paul had about ten minutes to prepare for the show, it all went incredibly smoothly. He did point out that he had Ed's camera script to work from, which made the whole process much easier. The camera script is a detailed list, explaining the shots for each camera, line by line of the show. It's far too complicated for me to understand but it looks a bit like this:

MCU KRYTEN ON 4
_____
                              KRYTEN
                              Well, sir, I think we have
                              entered a time-dilation
                              tunnel of incredible
                              complexity.

HIGH MCU LISTER ON 2
_____
                              LISTER
                              Complex, it's a cinch, I'll
                              get you through there, no
                              trouble.

WS STARBUG COCKPIT ON I
_____
                              RIMMER
                              I say we listen to the
                              square-headed one, let's turn
                              back while we can.

CU CAT ON 4
_____
                              CAT
                              We ain't going nowhere,
                              bud. We're locked out!

MODEL SHOT

It's as much as I can do to understand the plots, let alone how to make any sense of the camera scripts, so my understanding of the system is limited.

The atmosphere in the control room is always electric, thousands of voices at once, millions of buttons to press and hundreds of tellies to watch. In all the time I've been on *Red Dwarf* I've never been able to sit in the control room and watch a bit. I'd love to. I find it very interesting even though I don't understand it.

The two other good-fun-for-me episodes of series four were *Dimension Jump* and *DNA*, both because I appeared without the Kryten mask. In *Dimension Jump* I got to play Bongo, Ace Rimmer's superior. Instead of wearing four pounds of rubber I got a pair of Dennis Healey eyebrows and a bit of face-powder. Not only that, I got to proposition the great Ace Rimmer himself. Unfortunately Ace wasn't interested, and he didn't realize my bread was buttered that side.

In *DNA* I was out of the mask for much longer. This was the episode where Kryten gets transmogrified into a human being. For one episode. Just one episode. Not that I hate Kryten the mechanoid, don't get me wrong, but when he got zapped by the DNA machine, well, I thought my ship had come in.

This shows just how confused and under what delusions you can operate when you have your brains boiled weekly. It proves that actors can be, and often are, deeply sad individuals.

I thought that since we had recorded *DNA* as the last episode, it meant that Kryten was going to be human in the next series. At last Rob Grant and Doug Naylor had dug deep into their hearts and found a scrap of humanity there. They had decided to stop torturing the man in the rubber mask and let him be free, just a bit of powder and hair gel.

Looking back, I can imagine what happened. Rob and Doug were in their office late one night, the screen of their Apple Mac three-million-gigabyte computer casting an eerie grey glow over them.

'I know how we can really really get him.'

'Yeah, yeah, how?'

'OK, last episode we record, we'll come up with some way of turning him into a human.'

'So he doesn't have to wear the mask, yeah, yeah. Got it, got it.'

'And he'll think we've changed him into a human for ever.'

'Yeah, yeah. But come the first episode of the next series –'

'He's back in the mask.'

'Yeah, but better, with no explanation!'

'Yeah, no bloody explanation of any sort what-soever.'

'That'll really screw him up.'

On the pre-record day of the last show, I was in at the crack of dawn with Fiona and Andrea dabbing away with their glue brushes, but I was in good spirits.

'Oh, you are happy today, Roberto,' said Andrea. 'What are you doing after the series?'

'Going to Australia on holiday with my girlfriend,' I said.

'That's right, going to Australia,' said Andrea.

'You are a lucky boy,' said Fiona.

'He's a very lucky boy,' said Andrea. 'Isn't he a lucky boy, Craig?'

'He's a middle-class bastard, I know that,' said Craig as he sipped his coffee.

As you may have gathered, Andrea and Fiona tended to treat us like children. They spoke to us in loud, clear voices, somewhat like a primary-school teacher talks to her pupils. Andrea would get hold of your arm, shake it, and say, 'I want you back here for a make-up check after lunch, all right?'

Chris can impersonate Andrea very well. She is originally from Newcastle and it's an accent I can't hope to mimic. Not so Mister Barrie. 'Good mornin', Andy,' he'll say as he sits down in the make-up chair. 'How are you today?'

Everyone else is laughing except Andrea. She doesn't seem to notice his perfect reproduction of her every vowel.

'What's so funny?' she asks indignantly.

'I don't know, Andy, what's so funny?' says Chris in a lilting singsong Geordie.

'Oh, you're awful you are,' says Andrea, and proceeds to try and break Chris's neck as she sticks his hologramatic H on his forehead.

Chris's H is one of the daily rituals of *Red Dwarf*. It's made of thin plastic stuff which goes wibbly wobbly when you look at it from different angles. It's a bit like that stuff they make postcards out of in Spain, the ones with angels who flap their wings, or a

Jesus who winks at you. The H is applied to Chris's forehead with double-sided tape, special trick Sello-tape stuff which all costume and make-up people carry with them at all times. It's also called toupee tape as you can stick your wig down with it.

Chris has to sit in his chair and hold his head straight as Andrea braces herself behind him. They then fight for about a minute as they argue about it being straight or not, and finally they stick it on. Andrea pulls with all her might from behind, Chris leans forward with all his might from the front. At the end of a series Chris's neck is like Mike Tyson's, virtually thicker than his head. He strains every fibre in his neck just to stop his head from being pulled off. When it's finally applied they both congratulate each other on a job well done. 'An H of extreme beauty,' says Chris. 'An H stuck on with such aplomb, Ms Pennel, that it has to be seen to be believed.'

Chris then leaves the make-up room and has a bacon roll and a cup of tea or something. I assume he does that, I don't know, I'm still in the make-up chair being glued, prodded, padded and painted. It's not that I envy Chris his ten-minute make-up time, we all have our own weight to carry, but it always seems so short to me.

The fun part of that last day was recording the conversation between Kryten's three spare heads. It was very uncomfortable but great to do.

There had been times the year before when I had done a silly bowlegged walk, and put on a ridiculous

Hovis-advert-style Yorkshire accent in front of the audience between takes. I usually said something like, Oooh, I've just kacked me pants. By heck, that's good, robo kack, that's kack wi' nowt tekken out. It was obscene and cheap, I know, but cheap is my middle name and it got a laugh.

Rob, Doug and I had discussed this before the making of the series. I said I wanted to play Kryten's dad, an old-fashioned no-nonsense Yorkshire robot who thinks Kryten's full of new-fangled ideas.

The Grant Naylor genius machine got hold of that hack, cheap idea and turned it into a row of spare heads in a cupboard. One of which had galloping droid rot.

To get the scene to work I had to stand in a semi-crouched position and stuff my head through a hole. The front half of the shelf was then slotted into place. It was a bit like being in a set of medieval stocks.

It was as big a surprise for me to see the finished thing as anyone else. The wonders of modern TV technology! There were the three heads in a row, and spare head three grumbling away on the end.

After the last pre-record day I waited until I received the much-longed-for phrase, Robert is clear. All this means is I can rip the front of the mask off and run for the make-up room. Every day I wear the mask, I can always be found hanging around the floor manager towards the end of the shoot. He or she is going to be the first person to know when I can leave.

The director is in the scanner, which sounds like a

Red Dwarf prop but is actually a huge truck parked outside the studio. In the truck is a vast wall of TV screens, each showing a slightly different view of the same scene. The director, at this time Ed Bye, sits in there and somehow manages to make sense of the forty voices and twenty pictures he's looking at. On top of all this is the voice of the floor manager asking him, 'Um, Ed, Robert wants to know if he's clear.' Then the floor manager looks at me with that face, that wonderful smile that means only one thing: You're cleared, Robert.

I shout as I barge past technicians, cameramen with cups of tea, production accountants with clipboards and mobile phones. Everyone's face is a blur. All I can think about is getting the mask off.

I had learned by the second series that if I had been in the mask a long time, the glue around the nose and upper lip becomes very loose, if not unstuck altogether. If I grab the nose and pull it, it just rips off. This immediately allows me to breathe more easily, it allows me to scratch my nose and feel my face come back to life again. But this sort of behaviour isn't really encouraged by the make-up department. The glue is incredibly strong, and it is quite possible to tear your skin apart by pulling at the rubber if it hasn't more or less come away already. I have done this to the side of my nose once and it's very painful.

Andrea and Fiona set about my head with a vengeance, Andrea reminding me that it was the last one, that I was a free man, that I had finished another series of *Red Dwarf*.

The make-up removal is a much faster but still quite complex procedure. Andrea gives me two cotton-wool make-up-removal pads soaked in warm water, which I hold on my eyes. This helps remove the eye make-up and protects my eyes from the prosthetic-removal oil. Then they cut the top of my head open with scissors, rip the rubber bald cap open and let out the heat. At this point I have to be wrapped up warm, because the sudden change in body temperature makes me feel very cold. I always start to shiver at this point. It's an incredible feeling because after ten or twelve hours with your head encased in rubber, you do get used to it. This sudden change gives me goose-pimples all over.

Then they start sploshing prosthetic-removal oil between the mask and my face, and working from the forehead down they slowly and painstakingly remove it. They always finish under the chin and as the last bit of sad, old wrinkled Kryten drops to the floor, the liberation is complete.

I glance up into the mirror and see the sad return of my own face, which at this stage looks like a three-day-old used tea-bag. All I have to do then is wash and scrub and pick for a few days as I constantly find bits of rubber mask stuck to the back of my neck, or behind my ear, or somewhere. It really does take a long time to get rid of every trace.

So there I was, on the last day of the fourth series,

in the camera rehearsal, without the mask, as usual. It's a party atmosphere, the camera crew are all joshing, the sound crew are joshing, everyone is joshing except Ed Bye, who still has to make the programme work.

Suddenly it's the lunch break, and I walk out of the studio with the camera crew and the sound crew and the actors, out into the open air, around the studio lot, to the canteen. I've never done this before on a studio day. I always went up to my room and had a lie down. I can't eat with the mask on and it can be quite depressing watching other people stuff their faces.

The rest of the day went in a blur of happiness. When we had finished the camera rehearsals at about five-thirty, we all sat down for notes from Ed. I had never done this either. I would normally be in the make-up room at this time. Ed would come into the make-up room to see me separately and say, 'Right, chap, your entrance in scene six, make it funny, that joke on page thirty-five, make that funny, and generally, make it more funny, OK, chap?'

'Thank you, Ed.'

This day, however, I got to sit with all the cast in the audience seats and listen as Ed, Rob and Doug gave us their notes. These normally consist of hints about camera angles on certain lines, or when to turn in a scene. It's usually a technical thing, the camera can't get to us in time, or the boom operator can't get good sound if we are in the wrong place.

Then, and this day was getting better and better by the minute, I went to supper. I went along to the canteen with Chris, Danny, Craig and Hattie and we ate food. I sat there, no rubber, no discomfort, and ate food. Oh it was marvellous. About three quarters of an hour before we started recording I dawdled into the make-up department feeling very calm and suave. Normally I would have been sitting there for two hours by then.

'Oh look at Mister Cool,' said Andrea. 'Such a happy boy, aren't we?'

'Deeply happy,' I said. 'Deeply satisfied with my lot. Ahhhhhh.' I sat down and luxuriated in my face. I looked at it in the mirror in which Kryten usually stared back at me. It wasn't Kryten, it was my normal face. My normal, rather ugly bags-under-the-eyes face. As Fiona did my hair and powdered my nose, I started to get depressed. I think Kryten is a lot better-looking than me. He's got beautifully chiselled features, he's got a kind, but strong, face. I think I've got a face that looks like an uncooked Fray Bentos meat pudding.

Finally we were all in our costumes, make-up checks done. The audience were in, it was packed to the roof as usual. We had decided that as Kryten's change to human was a surprise, we didn't want to spoil it for the live audience so I didn't go on in the early introductions. The first ten minutes of the show we had recorded the day before.

The others went on to deafening applause, then the

audience settled down as the title music was played. The first ten minutes of the show were shown on the many televisions that hang from the studio ceiling. At the end of this section, Kryten becomes human, and you could hear the audience react. 'Ooooh,' they went.

Suddenly I became very nervous. One of the odd side-effects of wearing the mask is that I have zero stage fright when I'm in it. I suppose my brain and body have so much to put up with anyway that getting nervous is just too much extra activity to bother with.

I used to get stage fright when I first started performing, sometimes months in advance. There were times when I was preparing to do a cabaret show in a pub to sixty people when I wouldn't sleep for three nights before. I was convinced I would dry up, I would have uncontrollable adrenaline rushes, my heart rate would be over the legal limit, I was a nervous wreck. As soon as I went on the stage though, I was fine and of course the relief afterwards was enormous.

The fright gradually wore off as I did more and more performing, until eventually I did so much, I was on stage more or less every night of the week, that I would forget to be nervous. This can have a very bad effect. If you are too relaxed when you go on stage, you can dry up and forget things, sing flat, trip over and generally blow it. I discovered this to my cost on a couple of occasions and so decided that I should try and hype myself up before going on. I would jump up and down on the spot and make funny noises, shake my hands loose and try and get going. It was always worth it.

Being in *Red Dwarf* was so utterly different from going on stage in a pub that it's hard to imagine any link at all. When I am in the mask, and someone says to the audience, 'And here, as Kryten, is Robert Llewellyn!' I walk out in front of them already in character because there's nothing else I can do. It's not me they're seeing, it's someone else stuck on the outside.

As I was ushered into the first scene of *DNA*, where the newly human Kryten is on the medi bed checking himself out, I was more nervous than I had been in years. I was really aware of the live audience looking at me. I felt shy, I could feel myself blushing. Obviously a lot of them were thinking, Oh, is that what he looks like, what a shame, but most of the anxiety was coming from inside me. These people were seeing me for the first time. I felt so naked. Well, I *was* half naked, I only had one of those hospital gowns on which let your bum hang out.

The floor manager motioned me to start the scene and I could barely manage not to shake visibly. My mouth was dry and my hands were sweaty. It was just as bad as being under rubber only now I had no excuse.

Craig came in and as soon as we started the scene I was all right. This was the now-infamous double-Polaroid scene, where Kryten, as a human, finds he is still attracted to domestic appliances like Hoovers and washing-machines, except that mechanoid desire has now turned into a sexual one, and he's noticed some activity in his lower groinal area.

Once the show was under way, I had a great time, charging about avoiding the curry monster and not getting too hot. Of course seeing Craig get a face full of Vindaloo sauce was a wonderful, enriching experience.

It may have been the most comfortable *Red Dwarf* I was ever to record, but it was a huge disappointment for one particular ten-year-old boy. My nephew Ben had travelled a long way to see Uncle Robbie be Kryten. He sat in the audience patiently and all he saw was his boring old uncle wearing a funny suit. I don't think he's ever really forgiven me for that.

I felt sad during the party at the end of the show. All these people I had made friends with, and I would never see them again. Oh sure, I might come across them here or there, but you get close to them when you work so intensely. It was such a farewell sort of party, I danced a bit, had some sausages on sticks, and then crept out so I wouldn't have to say goodbye.

CHAPTER 6

On 15 January 1991 I set foot on some very hot tarmac in Brisbane, Australia. I'd just spent twenty-four hours inside a metal tube, sitting still. I was fine, it was a doddle, I thought nothing of it. It was just like an extra-long make-up session.

I was in Australia for three months, to meet Judy's family and see some of the country. I travelled from Brisbane up the coast of Queensland for a while, where it was even hotter, then down south to Sydney, and finally Melbourne. From Melbourne I visited the outback when I flew to Alice Springs to stay with friends.

I did actually meet one person in Brisbane who thought they'd seen *Red Dwarf*. It was shown on the ABC on a Sunday afternoon, so not exactly prime time.* One person who had seen it though was in one of the most far-flung places I've ever been.

The friends I stayed with in Alice Springs said that I should try to go and see Uluru, or Ayers Rock as we know it. It's seven hundred kilometres from Alice, or just down the road, mate, to an Australian. I inquired about hiring a car, or flying, or going on a coach, but on the morning of my departure a woman

* It's far more popular now.

rang the people I was staying with and said, 'Anyone there want to go to Uluru, mate? We've got a truck we need taking back there.'

An hour later I was heading out of Alice Springs in a two-ton, four-wheel-drive pick-up truck belonging to the Pitjanjara Women's Association. It had been left in Alice to have a service, and there was no one around to take it back out to the Pitjanjara women, except me.

It was fun to drive, but very slow. I never went above fifty miles an hour, and when the road you are on stretches dead straight, dead flat and dead hot as far as you can see, it can become a bit tiresome. After driving for four hours due south, I came to a garage. I stopped and bought water and a sandwich from a small roadside café. I didn't need to buy diesel as the truck had an eighty-gallon tank and a special reserve tank which held another fifty gallons. It also had a fifty-gallon water tank.

The area I was driving through is one of the hottest and driest on earth. A few weeks before I arrived an Aboriginal family had been driving across the bush when their pick-up had broken down. All three adults died of heat, exhaustion and thirst. They buried their child in the earth to protect it from the sun, and the child survived. A horrifying story, and hard to understand unless you've been there. The sun is so hot and unforgiving, it burns your skin in seconds.

The road came to a T-junction at the garage where

I stopped. One road went to Adelaide, two thousand miles south, the other went to Ayers Rock, four hundred miles to the west. I turned to a westerly direction and put my foot down. It seemed like I'd been driving all day already and I had a long way to go.

After about three hours I saw a sign which said CURTAIN SPRINGS ROAD STOP, TEN MILES. I decided to pull over there and have a stretch. It turned out to be a tin shack with a huge TV aerial, a couple of petrol pumps and a few broken-down old cars. The man who came out to greet me was straight out of a XXXX advert. Huge, fat and red-faced. He wiped his brow in an exaggerated fashion and said, 'Hot enough for you, mate?'

I asked how hot it was, and he said, 'Fifty-one degrees centigrade, mate?' That's about a hundred and thirty-eight degrees Fahrenheit.

'Hot enough for you, mate?' he repeated. It seemed to be his mantra. I followed him into one of the tin huts.

I pulled a bottle of near-frozen mineral water from the huge humming freezer cabinet, and noticed that the seal was already broken. I assumed he refilled them; not a lot of health-and-safety visitors to Curtain Springs, I guess.

'You a pom, mate?' he asked. I had been in Australia for two months and no one had called me a pom. I told him I was, and this led on to a discussion of the heat, the flies, the Bungs, which is the local red-neck parlance for Aboriginals. Delightful. He went on at great length about what to do if you break down. All the normal outback topics. Then he asked me what I did. As I stood in a tin shack, five hundred miles from anything other than sun-baked dust, what I did seemed peculiarly irrelevant.

'I'm a writer and actor,' I said, trying to sound butch, but sounding about as fey as you always do with an English accent in Australia.

'Oh yeah, you famous then?'

'No, no, not at all.'

'C'mon, what have you done? I might have seen it.'

'Well, there's this British comedy series called *Red Dwarf*.'

'*Red Dwarf*!'

'Yes, it's about . . .' but I never got a chance. I had met Pat, the Northern Territories' biggest *Red Dwarf* fan. The huge TV aerial by his shed was his only contact with the outside world. He could just about receive the ABC, Australia's equivalent to the BBC. On Sunday afternoons his wife, who I never met, had to man the pumps while he sat back and watched the programme.

'Never miss, mate, you smeg head.'

It took a long time to explain that I wasn't the Kryten he'd seen. He looked at me slightly sideways as I told him the episodes he'd seen didn't include me. At that time in Australia, only series one and two had been shown.

I left Pat and Curtain Springs and the flies and the heat, and drove for another six hours, dead flat, dead straight, dead hot. Suddenly the road had a slight bend and I caught sight of this magnificent red lump. After all those hours of flatness, Ayers Rock just traps the eye. I drove towards it for another half an hour before I reached the gates of the Uluru National Park.

I stood under the canopy of stars that night, stars like we in Europe cannot imagine. The rock seems to glow at night: it really is the most remarkable natural object I've ever seen.

I got back to England on 5 April and dived straight into rehearsals for a comedy lecture I was presenting in London. This was called *The Reconstructed Heart* and was a wry look at the male response to feminism from 1970 to 1990.*

I first performed the lecture at the London University theatre called the Bloomsbury. I had tried it out in Australia; the first reading took place in Alice Springs, in a kitchen, in front of twenty people, a couple of dogs and a six-month-old baby. Thank goodness it worked at the Bloomsbury. People laughed and *The Reconstructed Heart* was commissioned by Channel 4 as a comedy lecture to be broadcast on Valentine's Day the following year.

* In fact the final title is *The Reconstructed Heart, How To Spot The Difference Between a Normal Man and One Who Does The Housework, is Great in Bed and Doesn't Get All Iffy When You Mention Words Like Love and Commitment.*

In the meantime I made appearances in *KYTV*, where I was a roving reporter during a charity fun day, and I was hung upside-down and whipped by a woman in a rubber skirt.* As if that wasn't enough, I was mounted by a giant rabbit and I had to pour a bucket of water over my head. It was all good clean fun.

I also appeared in *Hysteria*, the AIDS benefit that Stephen Fry and all that lot organize each year. It was the same thing I'd seen Ed Asner and Jerry Hall doing the year before, and now I was in it. Oh swollen-headedness be mine! But no, the irony light was flickering.

It was great fun to do. I even met Hugh Laurie and we compared faces. Quite a few people say I look like him, including his wife! I don't think I do, but he is the one performer I can impersonate. We stood in front of a mirror and I did my Hugh Laurie impersonation. 'I say, that's quite remarkable,' he said, doing a much better Hugh Laurie impersonation.

In August I flew to Edinburgh to perform at the Assembly Rooms, where I was doing *The Reconstructed Heart* for two weeks. It was great to be back. It was only minutes after getting off the plane that I was in the Assembly Rooms bar, swapping humorous anecdotes and laughing loudly. I was only there an hour and I had a bad case of Edinburgh neck, craning

* Notice how, whatever I do, there always seems to be a rubber content somewhere.

every which way trying to see who was there, doing what, with whom.

The show went very well. It wasn't too tense, i.e., I didn't have to remember too many lines. Well, it was a lecture, and I had a nice lectern in front of me with all my lines on it. I gave up trying to remember a speech that lasts an hour and ten minutes. It made life so much easier to have a quick glance every now and then. Proper actors would not approve, but stuff them. Each day I tried new bits that I'd write in the evening, scribble on to the script and present the next day. This was a good way of trying out new jokes, some of which worked well and some died phenomenal deaths. I developed a question-and-answer session at the end of the show which really took off in Edinburgh and which I used in the televised version.

Back in London I did a special performance of the lecture at the Hackney Empire, a double bill with Cynthia Payne, the Streatham madame who was gaoled for running a house of ill repute which was full of judges and police chiefs, MPs and civil servants. I also spent a day driving a taxi with Dawn French in the back. I was a cabby in an episode of *Murder Most Horrid*. Dawn and I talked about setting up a special school where young men could be trained to be better lovers. She wanted to be headmistress.

While all this was going on, *Red Dwarf V* was brewing on the horizon. Was there going to be another series? Would I do it? Would any of us do it? The mystery had become a yearly tradition.

While I was preparing the lecture for TV, I learned that *Red Dwarf V* was on.

The read-through is often the first time we all meet up again. Sitting around a huge table with a huge pile of scripts in the middle. There's Chris Barrie with his mobile phone. Craig is wearing a groovy new jacket and Danny has a sweatshirt with the letters KMBBA★ emblazoned across the front. Hattie is wearing one of her stunning big red frocks. I am in sad old cycling trousers and a ripped T-shirt.

'You look like a tramp, man,' said Craig as he gave me a hug.

'I know, I'm really sorry, it doesn't matter how hard I try, I'll never be smart.'

'Middle-class bastard,' said Craig.

After the read-through Rob and Doug took me into their small annexe office for a quick word. I thought, Oh no, this is it, they have realized I'm crap and they're giving me the Spanish archer.† Tony Slattery has said he's happy to wear the mask and he won't complain.

'Bobby,' said Rob, 'we've just heard from Universal Television in Los Angeles that we are going to be making a pilot of *Red Dwarf* in January, and they want you to play Kryten.'

'Oh,' I said, 'wow.'

I don't think I said anything else at that point. I

★ Kiss My Big Black Ass.
† El Bow.

was so surprised at the whole notion. Doug explained that they were recasting the rest of the actors with Americans, but the producers in America really liked my performance and wanted me in it. My mood went from grim foreboding to swollen-headedness faster than a limp penis raises its purple helmet in a dirty bookshop.

Rob and Doug asked me to keep the whole thing quiet as nothing was that worked out and they didn't want to talk about it with the rest of the cast. I walked out of that office feeling fairly confused. Was this really going to happen? Was I really going to go to America and be in an American version of *Red Dwarf*? For the first time I think I actually became aware of irony control. I could almost see the big red light flashing, the men with the clipboards recording readings. Men with headphones flicking switches and giving concerned glances to the officer in control: 'We have a very high irony reading on subject Llewellyn, sir. He could blow.' I had to leave all my speculative thoughts to one side though, and get on with the job in hand. My comedy lecture.

We recorded *The Reconstructed Heart* at the Greenwood Theatre in London. It's where *The Jonathan Ross Show* comes from. The Greenwood Theatre is part of Guy's Hospital, and when you arrive there you wonder, Why did a hospital build a theatre, surely that's a bit odd? I asked someone who worked there, and this is the explanation, verbatim: 'Someone died and left a lot of money to Guy's Hospital, saying it was to build a theatre. An operating theatre or a theatre theatre. No one knew, they argued about it for years and eventually decided on a theatre theatre.'

Now forgive me, but I think that's a bit weird. If I left money to a hospital, I think I would have wanted them to build something useful for a hospital. Like an operating theatre. If I left money to a theatre, I wouldn't expect them to build a car park.

My mum and sister and brother and all my friends came along to the recording, along with about five hundred other people. It was very hard work,* but I was quite proud of it.

On 21 October, at six-thirty in the morning, I was sitting in a make-up chair in a location make-up lorry, parked next to a huge disused pumping station just below a flyover in West London having a new mask stuck on.

I had a strange feeling of *déjà vu*. Actually, it wasn't that strange, we were using exactly the same location as the year before. I did have a new make-up woman though: Nina Gan was working with Andrea on my head.

'You be nice to Nina, Robert,' said Andrea as soon as I had sat down.

'I'm nice to everyone,' I said.

'Yes, but you do moan a lot. Nina doesn't want to

---

* Now there's a luvvie statement for you. 'Acting is bloody hard work.' See *I, an Actor* by Nigel Planer.

hear you going on and on. Just try and shut up, that's what I mean by nice.'

The first thing I had to do on the first day was a long, complicated speech, while standing in a smelly, dripping, freezing-cold lower level of a leaking water-pumping station. I had only had time to glance at this speech before the first day of recording. I was utterly unprepared.

The new director that year was Juliet May. I didn't know her, she didn't know me. I could tell this by the fact that she said, very kindly and innocently, 'Just have a quick look at the script then we'll shoot it.'

Any proper actor would have been able to oblige, but Juliet didn't know she was dealing with the human sieve brain. Information can leave my brain like shit off a shovel. Luckily Kerry Waddel, who was assistant floor manager the year before, and floor manager on series five, knew me well. She started writing my speech down on a big sheet of card and held it up near the camera. There is a technical term for this sort of acting. It's called cheating, and I am quite good at it. We got the shot done eventually and the sequence became part of *Back to Reality*.★ We also shot other complicated sequences which were never used. As usual the old irony warning Klaxon was honking away unnoticed as Craig, Danny and I stood ankle-deep in stinking oily water, doing a scene which never saw the light of a flickering screen.

★ One of my favourite episodes of all time. Damn clever stuff.

One sequence which was used though was the chase and explosion scene from *The Inquisitor*. John Docherty as the inquisitor was chasing us through the endless walkways of *Red Dwarf*, firing his lethal time gauntlet.

Peter Wragg was on the case. He was carrying his trusty switch box and a reel of cable. 'We're going to have a fairly substantial explosion here, Robert,' he told me, pointing to a contraption on the floor. 'This is the scene where you and Craig are being chased by the inquisitor, and he blasts the other Lister.'

'I'm glad you understand the script, Peter,' I said.

'I don't,' said Peter, 'all I know is they want a bloody big explosion, so that's what they're getting.'

Craig and I, chained together at the ankle and wrist for added ease of movement, had to run along a narrow gangway, duck behind a big pipe, wait for a massive explosion and then run through the smoke, pick up the alternative Lister's severed hand, which I couldn't see, and run away.

It's so easy to explain, so easy to watch, so incredibly difficult to film. Everything always goes wrong. The explosion doesn't explode, the chains holding our ankles together trip us up, or break, or both. Remember, I was chained to Mister Craig Charles, head prop breaker of the northern hemisphere.

Somehow, after a long hard day, we managed to get the whole thing in the can. I was cleared and ran to the make-up truck.

'Where are we tomorrow, Andrea?' I asked, holding the soaking cotton pads over my eyes.

'Back here, I'm afraid.'

'What is it with Rob and Doug, man?' said Craig, who was seated beside me. 'What is it with this bloody pumping station? Have they got shares in it or something? Every year we come to the bloody pumping station and freeze our butts.'

'They're doing the shot where Lister has hung the inquisitor by a rope over the edge of a huge chasm,' said Andrea, completely ignoring Craig's complaints. 'They're filming way up in the roof, it's really dangerous, Craig, you'll like that.'

Andrea was right of course. She knows us all well. Craig's face lit up. There was danger in the air, he was going to be two hundred feet up above a concrete-and-steel floor, with no safety harness.

'Hey, great, I do all me own stunts, man.'

By nine o'clock the next morning, there we were, right up in the roof of this huge old building. A stunt man, dressed in the inquisitor's costume, was dangling from a rope at least a hundred feet above the floor. Just looking up at him from ground level made me dizzy. Then I was told I had to go up there as well, to shoot the final sequence.

I said to Craig, 'I don't do all my own stunts,' to which he replied, 'Middle-class wimp, stop moaning and get up there.' I always turn to Craig for emotional support in times of stress.

I have never suffered badly from vertigo. I've been

up the Empire State Building and the World Trade Center in New York, fine, no problem. I've been in a helicopter which hovered over Tower Bridge in London, exhilarating. I've looked over the edge of all sorts of cliffs and towers, easy. The only place where I have really gone dizzy and felt sick is halfway up that damn pumping station in West London.

I assume it was the mask, which restricted my peripheral vision, but as I climbed the last steel ladder up on to a wobbly moving crane I was shaking like a leaf. It did seem very high up, even though we were inside. How the stunt man hung from a rope up there I'll never know.

Then there was the night shoot. I had heard about the night shoot for a while. One of the pre-recording days was going to be a pre-recording night. We would start work as it got dark and work right through. Being night owls, Danny and Craig were happy to be up all night. Chris and I, however, were less thrilled. I like to get to bed at about ten-thirty with a good book, a mug of cocoa and a healthy erection. Chris can't be bothered with the book and the cocoa.

At about nine-thirty at night I arrived on the back lot at Shepperton, a small scrubby area of trees and man-made lakes which were once ornamental gardens belonging to the house. I wandered around, able to see because of the twenty arc lights which John Pomphrey had set around the grounds. Chris was recording the fight sequence for *Terraform*, where his

Self-confidence and Self-respect, dressed as musketeers, fight off the hordes of self-loathing, cloaked creatures with red eyes. It all looked amazing, smoke blowing through the woods, coloured lights shining up into the trees. I had a cup of tea with the technical crew who were standing around the tea table. It was great. This is what filming is all about, I thought, being warm and comfortable, but being outside, somewhere weird, at night. I asked the guys what the building behind us was. It was an old, broken-down greenhouse, overgrown with ivy.

'It's not real, Robert, it's a set,' said Chris Squelch, the man who lifted cameras about and drove the huge control truck. 'For a movie called *The Crying Game*.'

If you've seen the film, you'll know what the greenhouse looks like. It's where Stephen Rea holds the British soldier (played by Forest Whittaker) hostage at the beginning of the film. When I saw the movie a year or so later, the early part of the film didn't really work for me because I knew the greenhouse wasn't in Ireland, it was on a scrubby bit of old garden in Middlesex, and it wasn't a real greenhouse. It was made of balsa-wood and polystyrene.

Anyway, I couldn't hang around on the set having fun looking at fake greenhouses. This was *Red Dwarf*. I had to head for the make-up van.

The make-up van was warm and inviting. Andrea was in fine fettle. 'Good evening, Robert,' she said as I pulled open the door. 'Happy to be wearing the mask all night, in the cold, splashing about in freezing water?'

'That's comedy,' I said and took my seat.

Two and a half hours later I returned to the set in full Kryten. We recorded a lot of sequences for *Terraform* that night, and at about three-thirty in the morning we had to get into a punt on the lake and paddle through sheets of flame bubbling out of the water.

That's just the sort of thing that happens on *Red Dwarf*. You'll suddenly realize that you're covered in rubber and plastic, sitting in a leaking punt on a lake, with Craig Charles and Danny John Jules, both of whom are in high spirits, and you can't swim.

'You can't swim!' said Craig. 'You really are a wimp, aren't you, man?' he cried, giving me a friendly hug.

'I've tried to learn,' I said hopelessly. 'But it's true, I can't swim.'

'Come on, Dan, let's chuck him in, that'll teach him,' said Craig, jostling me towards the lake.

'Yeah, guy, that's a really good idea,' said Danny, without paying much attention.

Peter Wragg appeared dressed in a skin-diver's suit. He was joined by Chris Squelch from the camera crew, who is also a very experienced skin-diver. They sank into the muddy freezing water and held the punt steady as we stumbled aboard.

'Now listen, everybody,' said Peter Wragg, over the side of the boat. 'All around the lake we've got submerged butane-gas bottles. The gas bubbles up and is ignited by a fire-lighter. They're quite safe, but don't go too near them.'

'OK, Wraggy, man,' said Craig.

We started paddling out into the lake, and immediately, somehow, Craig was steering straight for a twenty-foot-high sheet of flame.

'You heard what the man said,' Danny hissed as the flames started to lick the front of the boat. Danny was sitting at the front and was obviously feeling the heat. We could hear the cries of warning from Rob, Doug and Juliet on the bank, but they fell on deaf ears. Craig was looking for a light for his cigarette, and there, in front of him, was the biggest light he'd ever seen. The lake looked like a Kuwaiti oilfield, flickering sheets of yellow flame tonguing the velvet night. As the boat floated serenely past the roaring pillar of flame, Craig popped a cigarette in his mouth and leaned over so that the boat was at its maximum tilt. I knew I was going to die. I was going to drown in a lake in Shepperton while making a British comedy programme. I was going to die because Craig Charles wanted a light. Then he sat back and exhaled a plume of smoke.

'Paddle on, dudes,' he said to me and Danny, who by now were both useless with laughter and fatigue. We eventually started paddling, but only in circles. We couldn't make the boat go straight. It seemed naturally attracted to the flames.

'We're heading for the flames again, guy,' wailed Dan from the front.

'Go to the left, Dan,' I said from the middle.

'Get it together, guys,' said Craig from the back.

He was now lying sprawled out in the soaking rear section.

'Try and paddle towards the camera light,' shouted Rob Grant from the bank. This caused more hoots of laughter. We were so tired and dizzy, paddling through a lake which seemed to be on fire, and we were told to aim for a tiny red light on a camera three hundred feet away.

Somehow Juliet and the crew managed to get some usable shots out of this sequence, but I don't know how. We were all out of control with hysterical laughter for most of the time we were in the boat. I completely forgot that I couldn't swim, I was having a great time paddling around this lake, occasionally seeing Peter Wragg's worried face as he swam through the murk keeping an eye on us.

The following week we started rehearsals proper with our new director, Juliet May. The first scene on the first day was set in the cockpit of Starbug. We sat in our positions with our scripts, Craig took hold of the newly devised Starbug steering column and it came away in his hand.

'I hardly touched it!' he said with offended innocence.

'That lasted a long time, guy,' said Danny flatly. For some reason this became the motto of series five. Whenever something didn't quite work, we'd all say, 'That lasted a long time, guy.'

As usual the schedule was gruelling, the make-up horrendous, and the scripts were killers to learn. That apart, the big difference for me during this series was my frequent visits to Rob and Doug's office after work. They would tell me excitedly how everything was going in Los Angeles.

'Looks like it's all going ahead, Bobby,' said Rob. 'There's this bloke called Linwood Boomer who's producing it. He's supposed to have written a script, and as soon as we get it, we'll let you see a copy.'

I couldn't really picture being in Los Angeles. I had been there on two occasions before, once on holiday, and once trying to sell scripts. I'd had a great time on both occasions, but I couldn't see myself living there. This was mainly due to the fact that I still had three episodes of *Red Dwarf* to learn and perform, and Los Angeles was a long way off.

On the daily journey between Islington, where I was living at the time, and Shepperton, I would listen to a tape of my lines on the car stereo. I would record it the night before, impersonating Craig, Chris, Danny and Hattie, and then leave a blank space for where my line was meant to be. Many's the time I've been driving around Shepherds Bush, or around the Hammersmith roundabout, mouthing Kryten's lines, and I've suddenly seen a bus driver or a cabby looking at me as if I'm some sort of nut. I have an involuntary head twitch when I do Kryten's speeches, which I imagine looks quite odd.

'See that bloke in front?' says a cab driver. 'Look at him, he's havin' a fit. Bloody nutter shouldn't be allowed on the road. I'll tell you who I had in here once. That coloured geezer,* the scouse one, Craig Charles, that's the one. Fuck me, he was funny. I tell you who I had in here once as well, some bloke who said he was the actor inside Kryten in that red whatsit space thing, the series, what's it called, red summat. I tell you what, he didn't look nuffin' like him. Lying toerag. Oh yeah, I get all sorts in here.'

I would pull to a halt in the Shepperton car park, next to Chris Barrie. 'Good morning, Chrisethony,' I'd say in an exaggerated not very good impersonation of Jimmy Savile, which I'd copied from Chris anyway.

'Good morning–ony, Bobethonython. And how are we this morningithon?'

'Very deeply well, Mister Barrothion, sir, and theyself?'

'Deep wellness is mine.'

I forget now where this odd mode of speech emerged from. I think Danny's inspired impersonation of Jimmy Savile may have had a hand in it.

'Here we are ladies – and – gentel – men, on the set of the Dwarf of the many Red of the many Dwarfs. Yes indeed.'

Danny would hold a bit of wood as a cigar, making various Jimmy Savile gestures as he spoke. Chris would throw his head back with pleasure, close

* This is how many cab drivers have referred to Craig over the years. I have only been in one cab once where the driver hasn't had Craig as a fare, and he was a novice.

his eyes and say, 'I'm there, Dan. To me, you are Sir James of the many Savilations.'

'What did I tell you, guy?' says Danny with a huge grin. 'I'm tellin' you this is a serious Jimmy Savile impersonation.'

'What are you on about, Dan?' Craig would ask as he looked for someone with a cigarette and a light.

'I'm doin' my Jimmy Savile impersonation, guy.'

'Dan, has anyone ever told you, you're cracked?' says Craig as he fiddles with a bazookoid gun. A toggle switch goes flying and lands with a clatter behind him. We all look at each other, waiting to see who's going to say something first, then in unison we all bellow, 'That lasted a long time, guy!'

The time when we are at our most unruly, the time when the four of us, who are, at a glance, four fully grown adult males, become unruly school-children is when we are in the Starbug cockpit during rehearsals. Somehow it's a bit like being in the class-room. Craig and Danny have been forced to sit in front because they are the bad boys. Chris and I, the swots of the class, are allowed to sit behind, but we are also often in trouble with teacher.

The conversation in Starbug can be quite mind-numbing, a mixture of Danny's showbiz facts, 'Prince is a seriously rich geezer, guy.'

My liberal wishy-washyness. 'Oh, I quite like Prince actually.'

Craig's piercing insights. 'You like Prince, Robert, man? So you like black culture, do you?'

'Oh yes,' I reply. 'Actually, I think I must have been black in a former life. Probably some sort of African prince, I would think.'

'Prince of Tossers,' says Craig, who, bored with the liberal, turns on the school prefect. 'Chris, man, how many cars have you got now?'

'Ah, let me see,' says Chris, sitting back comfortably and looking up into the roof. 'Well, there's the Bentley, the E-type . . .'

'The E-type!' screams Danny. 'That is a serious poom-poom wagon, man.'

'It certainly is, Danielski,' says Chris. 'Then I have the 1934 London taxi.'

'That's handy,' says Craig cheekily.

'It's a classic vehicle, Craig,' says Chris. 'Then there's the Range Rover, that's just a runabout, then there's the other Bentley.'

'The other Bentley!' screams Danny, who laughs richly. 'Imagine saying that, man. "This is my Bentley, and this . . . is my other Bentley." That has serious poom-poom potential, guy.'

Poom poom, executive poom poom, woofer, major woofer, bankable woofer. These are all terms I was, by now, *au fait* with. I would understand when someone said, 'That gag on page seven, bag it and bin it, guy, it's a ready-made cheque which I will pay into my already swollen National Woofminster Bank account.'

That means, roughly translated, The joke on page seven is very funny, so funny in fact that I know I will get a laugh, it will be simple to achieve a laugh, and I will store that laugh in an imaginary laughter bank, to call on in future when I do a joke which goes down the pan.

It's odd how certain words or phrases from the script can conjure up a whole experience or memory as well. For me, the word strawberry will never be the same again. I always remember trying to learn the replicator speech from *Demons and Angels*. I did learn it, but that was only the half of it.

Somehow this scene was a real pig to do, and when we originally shot it, in front of an audience, something went wrong and we had to do the whole thing again at a later date.

I had to use tongs to pick up strawberries, place them on the replicator and press a load of buttons. We would then get a good strawberry and a bad strawberry, as we would later get a good *Red Dwarf* and a bad one.

For some reason, talking and holding tongs, and remembering all the moves, pushed me to the limit. I seemed to be forever picking up strawberries and moving them about. Craig seemed to be forever watching me with great interest, then eating the bad strawberry, which was full of maggots.

'Hey, I'll eat me own maggots, man!' It was all a bit gross. I think *Demons and Angels* was another inspired bit of writing on the boys' behalf, but it was the hardest of the series for all of us.

When we were playing the low or bad version of

ourselves, we all got different costumes and make-up. Chris was in a kinky stockings-and-suspender Nazi whip-me fantasy, something he felt very at home in. Craig was dressed as a disgusting diseased pirate cowboy and Dan had grown monster sabre teeth. I, as irony control dictated, had an even hotter costume than normal.

My costume of series three, four and five was fairly respectably boiling, but my low Kryten suit succeeded in raising the human body temperature to previously unrecorded highs. I have never sweated so much, not in a Turkish bath, a sauna or the Australian outback. The low Kryten was very easy to play however: he was a bad-tempered old git, which is exactly what I was inside.

Conversely, the highs, or good versions of the *Red Dwarf* crew, were very comfortable to play. We wore loose-fitting golden robes and we moved about gracefully. Nevertheless, portraying the untimely and unkind death of high Kryten was one of the few times I suffered any discomfort at the hands of the great and good Peter Wragg.

'We're going to wire you up with some body impacts,' said Peter during a busy day's recording. 'Danny's got blood bags, but as you're a robot, you've got sparks.'

'Right, Peter,' I said, 'I'm with you, and, uh, how big are these sparks?'

Peter gestured a sort of fair-sized spark, which wasn't too big, but bigger than a very small spark.

'It's quite a spark, you'll feel it, but it won't hurt you.'

'Fine, fine,' I said, nodding in a butch, confident way. Peter and the special effects team wired me and Danny up, and we started the scene. When Danny's blood-bag body hits went off, the camera crew, sound crew and special effects team were all covered in blood. This was *Terminator II* meets *The Texas Chainsaw Massacre*. There was blood everywhere. Danny of course, being the trooper he is, gave good death. Then my body hits went off. Big sparks, shooting five, maybe six, feet out in front of me. Bop, bop, bop, on the chest area, bop, bop, on the stomach, and the one on the leg. Bop! Sudden pain. The one on the leg was attached to my long golden robe: somehow it had come loose and was facing sideways instead of front ways. The spark hit my thigh, just below the family downstairs waterworks department of the lower, front-mounted groinal-socket tummy banana.

It wasn't that bad, but as usual Peter Wragg was on the case. He takes his explosions and body hits very seriously. 'Yes, the spark went off sideways and hit your leg, Robert,' he said, examining the microscopic burn on my thigh, 'but it looked very good.'

Next, due to the fact that he was wearing hippie sandals, Danny got his toe burned by a fizzing atomic grenade, which the high Cat and Kryten took to be a beautiful glowing orb.

Then we had to shoot a sequence where the normal

Lister was on the run in a storeroom, trying to escape the low *Red Dwarf* crew. He stood next to a big case which the low Kryten was to come out of, manic and violent.

Inside the case, the special effects team had marked out two punch holes where I should aim my fists. I couldn't see Craig, but the idea was that I would punch through the holes, strangle him a bit, throw him down, then burst through myself, and, after doing a bit of comedy twitching, storm off.

Take one, I punch through the wall with all my might; I was wearing huge motorbike gloves with studs on them. I hit something hard and solid. It hurt like hell. It was the back of Craig's head. He went flying forwards into some barrels and whacked his forehead.

'Hey, I'm OK, man,' said Craig, rubbing both sides of his head at once. This time the crew joined in, 'He does all his own stunts.'

My hand was still hurting as we went for take two. This time the whole wall came out and I more or less fell on Craig. In the third take I did hit Craig on the back of the head, but I managed to strangle him as well, and by this time Craig was so bashed about he wasn't too bothered.

At the end of that day we were all a mass of bruises and minor burns, except Chris. Actually, I think he secretly wanted to get on his motorbike and ride home in his kinky low Rimmer outfit. But maybe that's just me projecting.

As the weeks wore on, the prospect of going to Los Angeles and recording a pilot version of *Red Dwarf* for NBC Television seemed to become more and more likely. On quite a few occasions I would meet up with Rob and Doug and find out what was going on. They gave me a copy of the script they'd received from America. I read it, it seemed very good, very like the *Red Dwarf* I knew already. It seemed close in its structure and gags to the first show made in Britain. It was on different-shaped paper though, and it had the legend BY LINWOOD BOOMER on the cover. I had a vision of Linwood: a short, tubby, fast-talking man with thick glasses. It was such a great name.

Right up to the recording of the last episode, nothing was certain. Then I got a phone call from my agent. Universal Television had made an offer. Shit, I thought, these guys are serious.

The final episode we recorded, *Back to Reality*, was one of the most enjoyable for me. For a start we got to work with Timothy Spall, a long-time hero of mine. Not only that, but I got to wear loads of different costumes, including the legendary Jake Bullet from *Cybernautics*.

I had to work opposite Dwayne Dibbley who is the funniest and saddest person anyone has ever had to look at. When Danny puts Dwayne's teeth in, I check my watch and give myself ten minutes clear. Dwayne makes me laugh out of control until I can't breathe. It was very hard for even Kryten to keep a straight face when Dwayne claimed to be the Duke of Dork.

'They can swivel on this mid digit until they squeal like pigs on a honeymoon.' One of my favourite lines. The human brain is apparently a massively complex system of neural networks, nerve clusters and grey squidgy stuff. It gives a human being an amazing ability to think, remember, record and create. Only it doesn't work for me when I have to remember a large number of *Red Dwarf* lines. My brain revolts against the deluge of information I am trying to force into it. Then a line like that comes along, 'And if those pen-pushers at City Hall don't like it, they can swivel on this mid digit until they squeal like pigs on a honeymoon.' I only had to read that line once and I knew it. I never forgot it, I can still remember it now. What mechanism takes place in the human brain which allows a joke to stay in there, and yet an explanation for time dilation goes in one eye and out of the other, never to leave so much as a skid mark on its way through the toilet pan of my mind?

I'll never know, but it's certainly one reason why comedy actors love jokes. They're much easier to remember. Although I have to admit, I am terrible at remembering traditional jokes. I start out well but then it all falls to bits: 'This bloke walks into a pub, oh no, no he doesn't, he's already in the pub, or is it a café? Look, never mind that, there's a man in some form of public environment, could be an office, let

let me think, oh no, then the punch-line won't work . . .'

I can go on like that for hours, then I forget the punch-line, or I give it out too early. There was a moment in series five where Rob and Doug used my rather odd line-learning technique in the show. It was during the final sequence of *The Inquisitor*, when Craig and I had frozen John Docherty, who was playing the inquisitor, and I was having to remember what I do next, a confusing condition only experienced when time dilation is an issue.

Usually, when we were rehearsing, and I was on the edge of actually knowing my lines, the floor manager would follow us around with a script. When I stumbled I would say, very fast, 'Don't tell me, don't tell me, I know it, I know it.' Then I would go quiet for a moment as my brain's memory banks sorted through a load of old rubbish, then I would say, 'What's the line?'

So in this scene, I ask Craig what I say next, then before he gets a chance to answer I say, 'Don't tell me, don't tell me, I know it, I know it.'

I think it's safe to say that this is the only time I've had a direct influence on a *Red Dwarf* script!

At the pre-recording day for *Back to Reality*, Timothy Spall had a problem. He walked into the make-up room, smelt the rubber mask, apologized and left. He came back a while later and explained that the year before he'd done a Christmas film with Dawn French, I think, where he played a pig. I'd never seen it but he told me he had to wear a full-face prosthetic mask day after day for three weeks. He found it so difficult to wear that he had vowed never to wear one again, no matter what. He was the only person I've worked with who truly understood what it was like. Everyone who sees me in it is sympathetic, but Tim Spall actually knew what it was all about.

The final recording was great fun. We'd had to pre-record quite a bit, so there wasn't so much to do when the audience were in. This is great for us as we finish early, not so much fun for the live audience who don't get to see so much.

There was a party that night, but it wasn't like the normal end-of-run parties, wrap parties they're called in the trade. I can't say wrap party though, it doesn't sound right coming from my mouth. 'Are you going to the wrap party, Craig?' I just couldn't do it, I'm not hip enough.

The reason the party was a bit of a flop was that we all knew we had to be up at the crack of dawn the next day. We hadn't actually finished. We had one more tough day in the studio. Pick ups, it was called. Picking up all the bits we'd failed to get during the seven previous weeks. This isn't surprising as *Red Dwarf* is a fiendishly difficult show to make. I have had this fact underlined after working on other shows which are so simple and easy in comparison.

That last day in the studio was a real killer. It seemed all the hardest parts of the series had to be done again, and some bits we'd never done had to be made for the first time. The studio was hot, I was hotter, and the day seemed to go on and on. Everyone was tired and towards the last shot of the last take of the last day I reached my last corpuscle of patience. We were all standing in the Starbug cockpit waiting to make an entrance into the rear section. We seemed to be waiting for ages, and the normal hectic banter between us had fallen to the odd phrase of encouragement.

'You'll be OK, man, one scene to go.'

'Let's hold it together, guys.'

Suddenly I shouted, 'Oh for fuck's sake, let's get on with it!'

Of course, with hindsight, it's clear how little this helps the situation. Every member of the crew was working hard, tired as they were, and were equally desperate to get the job done. But my eyes were really painful. They were tired before I had come into the studio, then to have to get up so early and have that much eye-irritating glue stuck so near your eyes can only be experienced to be understood. I don't recommend it to anyone. As regards knowing what wearing prosthetics is like, George Orwell was right. Ignorance is strength.

We got the last shot done. We were cleared. Everyone clapped and whooped, we'd done it, we'd made series five. The studio turned into a luvvie circus, everyone hugging and back-patting and congratulating everyone else. Then Craig had an idea. He got Rocket, the head cameraman, to line a camera up on to my face, then Craig got hold of my Kryten nose and started to pull, very slowly. Everyone was watching the monitors. Kryten's nose stretched and stretched, and his whole face became a pink cone growing out of mine. I had been so hot that most of the glue on my face was completely gone. The mask had stayed there out of force of habit.

Eventually the rubber gave way with a thwack and Kryten's face was removed. I'm embarrassed about what happened next because I'm a man and men aren't supposed to. It proves I'm a sissy and a wet wimp and a complete and utter luvvie. I burst into tears. Craig put his arms around me and led me out of the studio. In the corridor Chris gave me a big hug, as did Dan, and all I could do was blub.

In my dressing room, Craig kept his arm around me until the sobbing subsided and turned into laughter. The worst thing was, I knew why I was crying and I couldn't tell anyone. At that moment it felt like I had just been through a war with those three men. They had stuck by me, hour after hour, through all the smoke and explosions and screaming and laughs, the bad tempers, the hours of waiting and learning lines and standing in the queue in the canteen. All that time I knew that for some reason I had been chosen to go to America and make *Red Dwarf* there, and I hadn't told them. I felt like I'd cheated them. I felt like a heel.

CHAPTER 7

Qantas flight QF 47 rumbled along the runway, air brakes up, wing flaps down, and no doubt a lot of switch flicking going on in the cockpit. I was in the rear section, asleep. I was sitting alone, next to the window. I lifted the blind and was blinded, the light is so harsh and bright in Queensland.

I'd made it somehow. Only two days before I'd been weeping pitifully in the arms of Craig, now I was lifting my bag from beneath my feet.

'This is Wanda saying we hope you had a pleasant flight and that you'll fly with Qantas again in the near future. Please remain in your seats until the captain has switched off the seat-belt sign.'

When the planners designed Brisbane airport they made one small mistake: they put the runway in one field and the airport building in another. Once the plane has landed it has to go along the ground for about a mile and a half, but it's a pleasant trip. You see all sorts of sea birds and bushes, funny-looking trucks driven by men in shorts with long socks.

Judy met me in the airport and we drove to her favourite air-conditioned Italian coffee-house in Brisbane. We had both been busy all year. She was getting ready to go to Ethiopia to make a film for Channel 4, and I was going to America, for ever

That's how it seemed. We both felt our time together in Australia was precious. It might be the last time we were together for ages.

After two days, the phone started going.

'Hi, Robert, this is Mark Ivener,' said a voice so beautifully controlled it was hard to believe it wasn't computer generated. Mark Ivener sounded like Hal the computer in *2001*. No matter what was going on, he would always talk in the same lilting, soothing West-coast accent. 'I'm the attorney dealing with your work permit. Do you have a moment to talk?'

A moment? I had all day. I had an attorney, I couldn't believe it. I could picture him in his *LA Law* type office, the handmade suit, the Lamborghini in the underground garage. The huge house with the walk-around kitchen and the beautiful wife who did charity work. We'd all seen this man portrayed a thousand times in a thousand movies and TV shows. Mark Ivener, attorney, played by Kevin Costner. He gets the foreign actor the work permit, but then the actor moves into his life, his wife, his nightmares. *Visiting Performer* starring Kevin Costner, Michelle Pfeiffer and introducing, as the deranged madman, Robert Llewellyn . . .

'Getting you a work permit in the time allotted is going to prove to be quite difficult,' he explained. 'You will have to send me as much information about yourself as you possibly can.'

I was sitting in a suburban house outside Brisbane, twelve thousand miles from my flat. All I had with me was my little computer, a pair of shorts and some broken dark glasses. He wasn't kidding about it being difficult, but I don't know if he understood how difficult. Many Americans' grasp of geography outside their own borders is hazy at best, and sometimes astonishingly inaccurate. For all I knew, Mark Ivener thought that as people spoke English in Australia, it must be near England, or he may have thought I was Australian, or he may have thought I was an idiot.

With copious use of the phone I managed to get friends in London to go to my flat, find my cuttings file (a box full of old bits of newspapers and magazines), and send various bits and pieces, by expensive courier, to Los Angeles.

Then the phone started to ring again. It was Linwood Boomer.

'Hi, Robert, this is Linwood speaking, listen, Rob and Doug tell me you're still not sure about doing the pilot. I'd like to hear why you're having this problem, Robert. Maybe we can work something out.'

'Yes, that'd be good,' I said. I explained, 'It's kind of, a heavy commitment.'

I was referring to a section in the contract which dealt with how long I was under the control of Universal Television. Basically it was six years. They wanted me to sign something which would mean I might have to live and work in Los Angeles for six years!

'Six years seems like a long time to me,' I said.

'You know, in England we sign a contract for six weeks and we think we're going to miss a better gig.'

'Sure, sure, I understand,' said Linwood. 'But, you know, that part is a deal breaker.'

That was the term, deal breaker. That meant you could negotiate everything else, you could get a bigger limo, you could get a different make-up artist,★ you could get more money, that was easy. But sign for shorter than six years. No way.

'When people buy you in Hollywood, they buy you, Robert,' said Linwood, jokingly. I thought, That's the sort of humour that scares the shit out of me.

'I'll think about it and get back to you,' I said, and Linwood impressed on me the fact that getting back to him very soon would be very beneficial for the project, the people behind the project, and quite a sizeable proportion of the population of Southern California.

I had been worrying about the six year part of this deal ever since my agent first informed me, a few weeks earlier. I had spent a couple of hours on the phone to Nigel Planer, who I'd been working with earlier in the year. He was the only person I knew who'd been through the same thing. *The Young Ones* was taken over the Atlantic in the mid eighties, and

---

★ I had insisted on Andrea Pennel being my make-up woman in America. I thought the Americans would say no way and cite some union regulation, but it was no problem.

Nigel was the only member of the British cast to go. He had experienced a fairly hideous time, worried sick that he was going to have to stay there for six years with a group of people he hated who managed to make *The Young Ones* into a sort of grubby *Benny Hill Show*. He was hugely relieved when the pilot was a flop and he was released from his contract.

I'd been through a similar experience on a lower level many years before, when I was still working with my comedy group, The Joeys. A BBC director had seen a show we were doing and asked me to go along to read for a part he was casting. I had no experience at that time, I had no agent, I didn't know the first thing about the BBC. I went along and met the writer, a charming man called Howard Schuman, who wrote *Rock Follies* back in the early seventies.

They wanted me to play quite a large role, well, looking back I suppose it was the lead, in a new BBC drama set in a pirate TV station. To cut a long story short, I eventually said no. It was interrupting the work I loved with The Joeys, it was upsetting the group dynamics within the company, that's another way of saying we were dealing with professional jealousy in a mature and giving way. In fact, more importantly, I got the impression that the people behind the play just naturally assumed I'd jump at the part, like all actors would. Saying no was very hard. I felt physically sick afterwards, and I regret not working with Howard Schuman because I think he's good, but I was always glad I said no.

Now I was faced with the same decision, only on a bigger scale. Mind you, as I kept reminding myself, what a decision to have to make! Do I go to Los Angeles and get paid quite stupendous amounts of money doing a job I already do in England, live in a fab house in the hills, and drive a Ford Mustang convertible to work every day? Or do I go back to the rain and cold of recession-hit Britain?

Or, alternatively, do I work in Los Angeles, get mugged, get shot, go to an analyst, get ripped off, become a gym junkie, use steroids, pump up and turn into a sad sub Jean-Claude Van Damme and die of a heart attack while wearing a rubber head at the age of forty? Or do I go and live on a farm in Gloucestershire with a couple of pigs and a dog and live till I'm ninety-seven?

In Brisbane, Judy and I spent time with her family. Judy comes from a big Catholic family who, although not approving of our non-married, living-together-in-carnal-sin-type relationship, are very friendly and accommodating. This was to be my first Christmas in Australia. Christmas lunch was to be under the house and out in the yard, not on the beach, but I wasn't complaining.

Then, with Judy's departure to Ethiopia looming, we went for a week to a sea-front motel in Yamba, a quiet coastal town about four hundred miles south of Brisbane. We spent three days lounging around on the beach, going for walks along the river bank, watching pelicans and dolphins. It was so new and clean and tidy, our hire car was quiet and modern and clean, the sea was clean, the shops were clean: it was just like *Home and Away*.

Then, on the morning of the fourth day, at about five-thirty in the morning to be exact, the phone rang. The voice of the motel proprietor came on, 'Call for you from Los Angeles.'

'Hi, Robert, this is Linwood, how's it going?' said the super-clear voice on the phone. For a moment I thought, My God, he's come to Australia to get me, he's in Yamba with a gun!

'OK, Linwood,' I said, trying to wake up. 'I suppose you want me to tell you my decision?'

'Sure, Robert. That would be real good.'

I told Linwood how I was worried about living in Los Angeles, about being apart from Judy and my friends.

'I don't think you understand, Robert,' Linwood explained patiently. 'You are going to be very rich. If this series takes off, you more or less write your own ticket. You can pay for your friends to come visit, you can buy Judy a house in the hills to keep her happy. This is Hollywood, Robert. Stuff happens here.'

'Yeah, but six years,' I said feebly.

'Six years nothing. Do you know how much Ted Danson gets in *Cheers*?'

'Yes, but I'm never going to be Ted Danson,' I said.

'That's not the point. This is just to give you some

idea of what you could get if the show is a hit. Ted Danson gets over one million dollars an episode. He does thirty-six shows a year. Robert, you are looking at the prospect of earning some serious money here. Not only that,' he continued with barely a breath, 'I know you're really going to get on with the team we've got here. Some really great actors, really nice people who I know you're going to bond with. What it all adds up to, Robert, is being paid a heck of a lot of money for having a great time. Really, you should do it.'

'I have to ask the woman I love,' I said, surprising myself at the expression.

The woman I love rolled over in bed, looked at her watch, and said, 'Oh sign the fucking contract so I can get some sleep.'

'I'll do it,' I said to Linwood.

'You won't regret it. I'll get my people on to it straightaway. We're gonna fly you here first class, you'll get a limo at the airport, you won't know what's hit you. It's gonna be great, Robert, believe me.'

I was, I have to say, starting to believe him. I went out on our *Home and Away* sun porch, breathed the salty air deeply and felt tingly all over. The sun was just coming up over the Pacific. I watched a dolphin surface behind a fishing boat that was chugging slowly into harbour, the air was still cool and fresh, but with that special sea tang. It was drop-dead beautiful as I stared out to sea. It was across this ocean that I was going to go and change my life: become an American TV star, wear a rubber mask until I was forty-one, earn hundreds of thousands of dollars. Be rich.

Later that day Judy and I walked along the ten-mile beach which stretches south from Yamba. The sun was beating down but the wind kept us cool. I stood with my feet in the Pacific and said the word rich over and over again. I had never been rich, I had earned money, sometimes more than the national average, but for the vast majority of my adult life I had lived on virtually nothing. Subsistence living. Now, suddenly, in my mid thirties, I was going to be earning a huge amount of money.

I knew what real rich people were like. People with old money, seriously rich people, don't appear in TV sitcoms, they don't appear at all. They live in old houses in the Home Counties and shoot pheasants. Seriously rich people earn millions of pounds a year doing nothing, because they've got billions of pounds in the bank. I struggled to get my potential richness in perspective.

On New Year's Eve I flew to Melbourne and Judy flew to London to meet up with her film crew before flying to Ethiopia. I spent New Year's Eve with hundreds of Judy's friends at a warehouse party in Melbourne; she spent it in a plane waiting on the tarmac at Singapore airport.

On 8 January I caught the number 35 tram down the Saint Kilda Road, got off outside the American consulate building and picked up my passport. I turned the page and saw what had taken such a struggle to get. An H1 visa, allowing me to work in the United States for a period of six months from 10 January.

Early the following morning my mate Wayne took me out to the airport in his battered Honda. It was a great way to start a journey to immense, undreamed-of wealth; sitting on the ripped seat of a rust-bucket car with my bag stuffed on top of the kiddie seat in the back.

I got to the airport about an hour before the flight. I had a first-class ticket waiting for me. You don't have to hang around when you're on first class. A nicely dressed young man carried my one small bag to the plane with me. I only had to carry my ticket. I was shown to a huge leather seat up in the nose bit. It was like an armchair. I sat down and was offered champagne. I don't normally drink, but this was too much, how could I refuse? Before I'd got over the bubble effect of the champagne, the plane started to move. This is the life, I thought: get on the plane, plane flies. No hanging around watching people try and stuff too much luggage into the overhead compartment.

I also discovered why they put the first-class compartment at the front of the plane. It's about ten times smoother than the back, where I normally have to sit. You can barely feel the plane moving. Then I discovered my toiletries bag. You may be able to tell from this that I love flying, which I do, but this was the best. A little leather toiletries bag, full of the best gentlemen's bits and bobs on offer, aftershave, face-cream, mouthwash, toothpaste, toothbrush, not a little fold-up one, a posh, proper toothbrush. Nice pongy soap, a little flannel, a plastic thing for getting fluff off your clothes. I was in heaven.

There were only two people in the first-class compartment, me and an orthodontist from Beverly Hills who had been visiting his daughter in Sydney. He told me I had potentially good teeth, but that if I went to see him, he could give me star-quality teeth. I said I didn't like perfect white teeth, I thought they looked fake. He said he would hand sculpt my teeth so they would look naturally perfect. The orthodontist and I had three members of the cabin crew to look after us, so they weren't exactly stretched.

The plane landed in Los Angeles two hours before it had taken off in Melbourne. I started the journey at twelve-thirty in the afternoon in Melbourne and arrived in Los Angeles at ten-thirty in the morning of the same day, but I'd been flying for eighteen hours. I stood in the immigration queue scratching my head, with that special expression which only happens to people when their internal body clock has completely blown a fuse. No amount of watch gazing or mental mathematics can alleviate the hollow, burned-out feeling you get after a long-haul flight. I love that feeling; it's better than taking drugs. I was completely out of it as I handed the official my passport. He looked at my work permit, looked at me, looked at my work permit again, smiled slightly and said, 'Welcome to the USA, sir.'

'Thank you,' I said.

'You're welcome,' he said, and I knew I'd arrived. As I walked out into the main concourse there were three hundred limousine drivers standing behind the barrier, each of them with a card bearing someone's name. I scanned the cards, but there was nothing that looked anything like Llewellyn. I was prepared for something akin to Llewellyn, like Lew Allyn, or Lew Ellen. My name has been spelt many different ways over the years. But there was nothing.

I kept going, past the throng of people waiting for passengers to emerge, and sat on a seat in the waiting area. The shock of America is always pretty intense, I find. It operates on a higher level than any other country I know. Anything can happen in America. You can make it. If it seems hopeless in Europe or Africa, when you arrive in America you know immediately it is possible.

'Mr Llewellyn?' asked a deep male voice.

I looked up into a sun-tanned face with perfect teeth and a carved sculpture of super-shiny hair on top.

'Yes.'

'Hi, I'm John, I'm your driver at this time. Would you like to follow me?'

I stood up to discover that although John had a wonderful deep smooth American voice, he was a little on the short side. Still, he wasn't letting that hold him back.

He picked up my bag and started making his way through the crowd. I was on my guard. This looked like the oldest trick in the book. Read the label on my luggage, ask me to follow him, then pull a gun on me in the car park, put me in the trunk of the limo, drive out to a desert ranch full of psychopathic killers, nail me to the floor and gang rape me to death over a period of three weeks.

John walked to a huge, and I mean *huge*, joke of a car. It looked six cars long, an absurd long black thing with about fifteen windows down the side. It was *the* cliché, it was the stupid stretch limo that is so embarrassing now, so out of date. Let's face it, a stretch limo is now, and always will be, a tosser's car.

John popped the trunk,★ put my bag in and opened the door for me. I was sleep-starved and feeling so weird that I couldn't help giggling a bit. I almost expected to see Michael Douglas sitting in the back, having a blow-job and buying Rio Tinto Zinc like it was going out of style. He'd be wearing a five-thousand-dollar suit, with his hair slicked back, he'd be Gordon Gekko.

'Robert, I want you to find out everything you can about Universal Television while you're there, I want to buy them out, I want to suck them dry, chew the fat out of the motherfuckers. I want to own their goddamn balls!'

'Yes, Mr Gekko, sir.'

★ Oh yes, I know all the expressions. It means, open the boot.

The limo was empty, huge and lonely-looking.

'Can I sit up in the front with you?' I asked rather sheepishly.

'Sure, Bob,' said John. No English person could call you Bob that quickly. I slipped into the spacious front seat, John started the huge car up and we hissed along the concrete roads.

'I had Ellen Barkin in here yesterday,' he said as we pulled out of the airport on to a huge five-lane freeway. 'She's a very very beautiful lady, and very charming.'

'Is that right? Yeah, I've always had a soft spot for Ellen,' I said, settling into the huge comfy seat and slipping on my dark glasses.

'Of course one of the perks of this job, Bob, is that I get to find out where everyone lives,' he said. 'I could take you to Ellen's house, introduce you maybe?'

'Oh yeah,' I said, suddenly panicking again. He had to be a serial killer, he knew where the stars lived, he kept a little black notebook next to a knife with a jagged edge. I would be the only person who could save Ellen. I'd run to her house, a police helicopter shining a light on me from above. I'd fight John to the death. I'd be injured, she'd visit me in the hospital, the black doctor would say I might pull through, Ellen would cry, we'd kiss. Aaaargh!

Within minutes of being in Los Angeles I had slipped into movieland. Everywhere I looked seemed so familiar, and although I'd been there on two previous occasions this familiarity wasn't from past experience. It was from the movies, the thousands of films we've all seen, filmed on the streets of Los Angeles. Tall palm trees, wide roads, absurdly stretched limousines. Big pick-up trucks with massive tyres, convertible Rolls-Royces with the roof down, bust-up old Buick station-wagons full of migrant workers wearing blue nylon peak caps.

We drove over South Central LA at speed. It doesn't look like much, row after row of red-roofed houses, the odd palm tree, and every few miles a massive building with no windows which is an air-conditioned shopping mall. In the far distance the gleaming, glittering towers of downtown LA.

By now John had found out all about me. 'So, what's this series you're making?' he asked.

'It's not a series, it's only a pilot, it's called *Red Dwarf*.'

'*Red Dwarf*?'

'Yes, that's right.'

'*Red Dwarf*.'

'Yes, it's about a spaceship.'

'So it's not about dwarfs?'

'No, it's set on a spaceship, three million light-years from earth, going the wrong way.'

'*Red Dwarf*.'

'Yeah, that's right.'

This was a very American phenomenon. There was something about the title that a lot of Americas couldn't quite latch on to. They are terribly verbally right-on there, and using a term like dwarf makes them flinch. It's a bit like us using the term spazzo, or pouff. It's just not done. If an American actor said to you, 'I appear in this show called *Red Spazzo*,' you'd blanch a bit, wouldn't you? I would.

'*Red Dwarf*.' John was still stuck on this.

'That's it,' I said.

'Actually, Bob, looking at you, you are perfect for a project I'm working on.'

This was it, I thought, he was a psychopath, his project was my grisly murder.

'It's a movie about a pool-service operative. He goes to all the stars' homes and cleans their pools, and he has sex with all these women. I thought about casting him as French, but I think English would be brilliant. The project is with Ted Rinvalklatz, you know, who did *Bunny Killers* last year. May I send your agent a script?'

'Sure,' I said. I gave him my agent's card. We drove through Hollywood, across the hills and into the valley. This was the home of Universal Studios, where you can do the Universal Studio tour and see *Miami Vice* shoot-outs and Jaws comes to try and eat you.

We drove up a steep tree-lined drive and pulled up in front of the Universal Sheraton Hotel. Immediately there were smartly dressed men opening doors and trunks and palms as I carried my own very small bag into reception. I bid John farewell. He told me to expect his script at any time. I'm still waiting for it.

I checked in and got in the lift with a huge man in a suit and a very small blonde woman. The woman was Dolly Parton; she smiled at me. I didn't know what to do, I was tripping with exhaustion.

'Oh, hi,' I said. 'It's great to meet you.' Dolly smiled again, the door opened on the twelfth floor and I fell out.

My room overlooked a six-lane freeway and a swimming-pool fringed with lanky palms. I sat down and calmed down, the January sun was hot through the window, I had to try and stay awake until night-time or the jet lag would last weeks, and I was due to start work two days later.

I picked up the phone and dialled a long number that Judy had faxed to me from Ethiopia.

'Hello . . .'

'Can I speak to Judy –'

'Hello . . .'

'Hi, can I speak to Judy Pas –'

'Hello . . .'

'Yes, can I –'

'Hello . . .'

This went on for about three or four minutes until I could hear the phone being thrown down, then I waited a bit longer and suddenly there was Judy on the line. She was in Africa, she was having the time of her life, she was OK.

If by any chance you win the pools, or your Premium Bond comes up, and you get depressed because money doesn't bring you happiness, and you want to get rid of your money ... if you feel like that, here is a very good way of getting rid of quite stupendous amounts very quickly. Fly to Los Angeles, first class, Qantas, via Melbourne, that'll use up a fair bit, I would think. Then check in to the Universal Sheraton Hotel, call the Hotel Gohar, Gondar, Ethiopia, and ask to speak to Len. There won't be anybody there called Len, but they'll go and have a look for you anyway. As they look, you will be paying top dollar to listen down a phone line to the sound of Africa. Judy was OK, I was relieved. I fell asleep for what felt like a week.

The following day I met Andrea. She was with her boyfriend who was going round the world with her on a much-longed-for holiday. We met up in the lobby and drove into the valley to a special effects company that were making the new Kryten mask and costume.

The company was situated in a large industrial complex, the sort of place where Mel Gibson finds a heroin factory and shoots lots of stunt men.

The special effects boys were great, so like their English cousins, enthusiastic and fast-talking, living in a world of in-jokes and technical explanation.

'We are going to be doing everything in our power to make sure you are really incredibly comfortable, Robert,' said a man with a beard. 'So first we need to do a full body cast.'

In an effort to make me incredibly comfortable, I had to stand and be covered in plaster-of-Paris bandage again. The glamour of first-class travel and luxury hotel suites was suddenly knocked into focus. I was here to work, I was here to wear rubber, and there was no way of getting round that.

As I stood still I started to take in the surroundings. This was the company who made Spock's ears, fazers which could be set to stun, the little flip-top box that Captain Kirk asked Scotty to beam him up with. They made the weird wrap-around glasses for the black guy in the new *Star Trek*, which I haven't seen. They made guns and spaceships and all manner of weird bits and pieces for dozens of movies.

A man who looked like he was in *Easy Rider* entered the workshop. He was going to make my new mask. I got very involved in the discussions as to how it should work, how much of my face should be exposed, and if I could keep my own nose.

The battle of the mask was to continue for many days, but the man who made my mask, who I only met once, was a real genius, and a fast genius.

When Andrea and I got back to the hotel that evening Rob and Doug had turned up delirious with jet lag. They had been working flat out on editing the British series so they were tired before they set out. They sat in the lobby of the hotel, drank large schooners of lager, and grinned at everybody.

'It's amazing . . . I think,' said Rob.

'Yeah, no, yeah,' said Doug.

On Monday morning the cast and crew of *Red Dwarf* gathered inside the vast studio of Stage 43,

Universal City Studios. The space was twice the size of Shepperton, which is big enough. The sight that made us gasp was the set, an *exact* replica of the British set. The floor plan was the same, the fittings, everything. It was absolutely remarkable.

A man of at least six-foot-eight walked up to me. He looked like an ex-basketball player; he *was* an ex-basketball player, and the stage manager. He shook my hand firmly and introduced himself as Elvin Ivory. I followed his huge long strides outside into the weak morning sun.

'I'm going to show you your parking space, Robert,' he said, as if I was an unruly kid at kindergarten. We walked across a huge parking-lot and he stood in an empty space in the middle. 'This is your parking space. If anyone else parks here, you come and tell me, and I will personally kick their ass. And if you park anyplace else, I will kick your ass. You understand?'

'Yeah, sure,' I said, trying to sound local and cool. 'There's only one problem.'

'What's that?' snapped Elvin.

'I don't have a car.'

Elvin was silent for a moment, he chewed his lips, then he said, 'Robert, I don't give a damn if you have a car or not, this is your space and if any other mother parks his car here, I want you to tell me. You understand?'

'I understand, Elvin,' I said.

I followed Elvin back to the studio. As we walked

down the canyon between the huge buildings, he pointed to a smaller building which looked like a block of flats. 'That's your dressing room over there. It's got your name on the door, Robert Llewellyn.' Elvin clearly didn't leave anything to chance. He was to continue to remind me of my name at regular intervals.

In the studio more and more people were gathering, men in suits mingling with scruffy-looking arty types. At that point I had only met Hinton Battle, the actor who was to play the Cat. His similarities to Danny were amazing. He was an actor and dancer, he'd been in dozens of Broadway shows, he'd won awards, worked with Diana Ross, all that kind of thing.

A thin man shook my hand, 'Hi, Robert, I'm Chris Eigman.' He had one of those sharp, funny, what I take to be New-York-intellectual accents. Chris, I discovered, is from Colorado, and he was playing Rimmer. I immediately warmed to him. He looked like an alternative Rimmer. Good casting, I thought to myself.

'Hi, Robert, welcome to Hollywood, I'm Linwood,' said Linwood Boomer. He wasn't short, or fat, he didn't wear glasses, he was a handsome, athletic-looking Californian. He shook my hand vigorously, I stared into his unusually bright blue eyes and wondered if his name really, really was Linwood Boomer. I always had a suspicion his name was Pete Jones or something, but a daft Hollywood agent had told him a name like Linwood would get him more gigs. Linwood used to be in an American series called *Little House on the Prairie* where he played a blind boy. His eyes are so bright blue it was easy to see how he got the part, you can never quite believe he is looking at you.

'Meet Craig Bierko, he's playing Lister,' said Linwood as he guided me towards a tall handsome man who I'd taken to be the director or a writer or someone like that. Certainly not Lister.

'Hi, Bob,' he said. 'Great to work with you, I've watched all the *Red Dwarf* series, I think you do an incredible job.'

So this was Lister, a tall handsome white man. When I had discussed this with Rob and Doug one evening in their office in Shepperton, they had been under the impression that Lister was going to be a short tubby Hispanic actor. That seemed to fit the bill, but presumably the Americans had worried that portraying a Hispanic man as a dirty, lazy, but very humane slob would create a negative reaction in the Hispanic community.

In the car park earlier I had walked past a glamorous woman with a lot of hair. Big hair, as I discovered it was called. She smiled at me and I felt flattered that someone so good-looking would even notice me. Suddenly she was standing in front of me shaking my hand. 'Hello, Robert, I'm Jane Leeves,' she said in a husky English accent, 'I'm Holly.'

Jane had lived in Los Angeles for ten years. She

was appearing as a regular character in *Murphy Brown*, a sitcom that gained international notoriety when the lead character, played by Candice Bergman, criticized the vice-president, Dan Quayle, during the run-up to the election.

My head was spinning with all this new information and these names, which I had to try and remember. Naturally, I managed to get the whole thing utterly confused. The cast stood in a small circle and I said everyone's name and pointed to them. 'Hinton, Jane, Craig, Chris.' I got Craig and Chris the wrong way round. I was so confused about the fact that they had the same names as their English counterparts my brain had gone on short time and I had decided that the coincidence was too great: it must be Rimmer played by Craig, and Lister played by Chris.

'I'm Chris, that's Craig,' said Chris Eigman patiently. He patted me on the back, 'You're confused, aren't you, Robert? But you're working in Hollywood now. It's important you remember everyone's name. I'll be testing you from time to time.'

People started to sit down around a long table in front of the set. Most people seemed to know where to sit, but I couldn't work it out so I hovered about, looking around for help. Elvin noticed this and pointed to a canvas director's chair with my name emblazoned on the back in red appliqué. 'Robert Llewellyn,' he said as he tapped the chair. I couldn't believe it! I had my own chair with my own name on the back, like in Hollywood. I *was* in Hollywood.

I sat down but kept turning around to look at my name. I showed Rob and Doug, who were sitting down the other end of the table. They stood up and showed me theirs; they had their own chairs too. The only difference was that theirs stood a good five inches higher than mine. There was already a hierarchy: the actors got the low chairs with their names on, the writers and producers and directors all had higher chairs with footrests.

'Good morning, everybody, and welcome to Stage 43, Universal City Studios, where we are going to make a pilot episode of *Red Dwarf*,' said Linwood in his soft, undulating tones. 'We are all going to have a great time here, this is a fantastic script, it comes from a great series which is a real big hit in Great Britain, we've got a fantastic cast, you guys.' He looked along the side of the table where we were sitting. 'Craig Bierko, Chris Eigman, Robert Llewellyn, Jane Leeves.' There was a huge round of applause from everyone. Rob and Doug joined in slightly later but with no less enthusiasm.

Linwood continued, 'A great director, Jeff Field.' He looked at a quiet-looking man with a beard who nodded and smiled, he got another round of applause, not quite so big as ours. 'And a great crew.' About fifteen assorted people whooped and clapped vigorously.

'Well, all right!' said Linwood, rising to the occasion. 'I know we're all going to bond real good, and really have a great time, because if we have a great time, we'll produce a great product. And that's why we're here, people, to produce good television, *Red Dwarf*.' Even Linwood said *Red Dwarf* a bit like John the limo driver. 'OK, so let's read the script, then we'll have a talk, get to know each other, and have lunch.'

My smile was fixed to my face. I told myself quietly, These people are clearly mad, they all clap each other but we haven't done anything yet. Stay calm, you're only here for three weeks, you haven't actually signed your contract yet, breathe into the anxiety. I glanced to my right to see Craig Bierko looking healthily depressed. Maybe they're not all mad, I hoped as I picked up my script.

As we read, the banks of men in suits sitting in the audience seating laughed very supportively during the funny parts. The director laughed convincingly, but automatically, at every potentially amusing moment. We had to wait every now and then for Linwood Boomer's long, languorous, Ahaha ha ha.

For the first time in my *Red Dwarf* experience though, I was the old-timer. I knew my character backwards, while everyone else was struggling with theirs. As soon as we'd finished reading through the script, the cast gathered around the craft-services table.

Craft services is catering to you and me. At the BBC this might sometimes stretch to a coffee machine and a pile of plastic cups, sometimes even one packet of biscuits. In Hollywood there was always a huge table freshly stocked with regular coffee, decaff coffee, fifteen different sorts of tea, herbal and regular, Danish pastries, doughnuts, a massive bowl full of candy bars, bowls of fruit like they have in adverts, chewing gum, bubble gum, lollies, mints, muffins that are like small Christmas cakes, and a fridge full of every sort of soft drink, fruit juice, cola and mineral water you could imagine. The table sagged under its heavy burden, and as soon as we'd demolished one pile of food, it was mysteriously replaced by someone from craft services.

'So what d'you think of the script, Robert?' asked Hinton. I was just about to speak when I realized the whole cast were standing around waiting to hear what I had to say.

'Oh, ur, it's ur, yeah, it's good.'

'C'mon, it's crap, isn't it?' said Craig Bierko.

'Well, it has room for some more gags,' I said politely.

'Like about ten square miles,' said Chris Eigman. 'C'mon, people, let's face it, we've got a turkey on our hands.'

'Oh no,' I interjected, 'it'll be OK, look, the boys are here.' I pointed to Rob and Doug who were talking to Linwood Boomer and Jeff Field, the director.

'Is that Rob and Doug?' asked Hinton. I nodded. 'Which is which?'

'Rob is the one wearing the weird cowboy boots

who's smoking and talking quite a lot. He's sort of harsh and cruel on the outside, but actually I think there's a very caring person trapped inside somewhere. Doug is the one with the limp who is talking less, but listening very carefully. He's more caring and considerate at first glance, but I have the suspicion he is an absolute rock on the inside.'

It was like a scene from a thirties backstage movie. The cast were all grouped around to hear what I was saying. I was almost expecting Mickey Rooney to walk in at any moment and say, 'C'mon, guys, let's do the show here!'

We had lunch together in a huge canteen which was miles away on the other side of the lot. To get there we had to walk through the public part of the studio complex, the Universal Studio tour section. It was like working backstage in a theme park because that is essentially where we were. Every ten minutes or so a tractor pulling five hundred people in open-topped trailers would rumble past the studio door and we would hear snippets of studio history. 'On the left is the studio where, in 1953, Clint Eastwood made his first appearance in . . .'

The canteen was not full of movie stars, but every now and then someone would walk past who I recognized from some sitcom or other that had been shown in England. Of course, being proper actors, my fellow cast members knew who everyone was, what they were in now, what they had been in, what they were hoping to be in, how much they got paid, which agency they were in and which team they batted for.*

We spent the afternoon blocking out each scene in the most relaxed and happy manner. The whole set-up was so calm, our every whim was catered for, and there was absolutely no pressure on us to do anything. Jeff Field came up to me at one point as I was trying to learn the first couple of speeches I had to do.

'Robert, maybe we could go through this opening scene at some point, you know?'

'Sure, sure, sure,' I said as I jumped up, my normal reaction from three series of *Red Dwarf* in England.

'No no, there's no rush, you come over when you're ready,' said Jeff. I was slowly learning that all the hierarchies I was used to did not apply in America.

On the set of a British TV programme, the director is the boss, everyone works around him or her. In America, it's the producer, who is often one of the writers as well. Linwood Boomer was that man. Jeff was just the director and seemed to be more or less at our beck and call. The actors seemed to be the ones in charge.† When we'd been over the show once,

---

* An Australian expression referring to a person's sexual orientation. 'Don't fuss with him, mate, he bats for the other team,' was a snippet of conversation I heard between two women in Melbourne once.

† Which of course contradicts the hierarchy of the chairs with our names on the back. High chairs for crew, low chairs for cast. Maybe in America, the lower your chair, the higher your status. I expect Mel Gibson and Tom Cruise have a small flat cushion to sit on between takes.

Linwood showed up and we all went through it again for him.

He looked like a worried man when it was over. He looked yet more worried after Chris Eigman and Craig Bierko both had a little word with him. Quite rightly, they both thought their characters were being short-changed. I kept quiet because from where I was standing, Kryten had all the best lines, the best gags and the best routines. The other unexpected bonus was that I knew most of my lines already because I'd learned most of them before. This was the odd thing about the script: although it did have Linwood Boomer's name on the cover, I recognized a lot of the lines from the first episode of the British version. It was an adaptation of the original script but, as seems to happen so often, it had lost some of its original sparkle.

The first week was spent very calmly going through the script, blocking out each scene, eating Danish pastries and drinking coffee. At one point when I was making an entrance into the sleeping quarters, Jeff Field asked me why I kept ducking as I walked in through the door. 'Don't get me wrong, Robert,' he reassured me, 'I like it, it's cute, but why do you do it?'

I explained that I had to or I would knock my head on the top of the door frame. Jeff and I stood under the entrance: the top of the door was a good six inches above my head. I had been on the set about three days before I realized it was about half as big again as the British set. It looked exactly the same, but it was bigger. This was a metaphor for the whole experience for me: I was in a country where everything was bigger and different, but I still behaved the same. It was going to take me a long time to adapt.

In the evenings after rehearsals Hinton and I would generally go to the twenty-four-hour gym that was just down the road, have a big workout and then go to a diner and stuff our faces with high-fat food laced with colourings, flavourings and E numbers.

Hinton was great. He had been born and bred on an army camp in Kansas, his father a middle-ranking military man. Hinton hadn't heard the word nigger until he went to Washington when his dad was posted there. He was called one by a black man on the street.

We discussed the possibility of the series going ahead, and what we would do.

'I'm happy to live on the Coast,'* said Hinton, 'I've been in New York too long.'

'I don't know if I'm happy about it or not,' I said.

'Hey, man,' said Hinton, 'get in touch with your feelings.'

I tried to. I said, 'Well, I don't like London that

---

* The Coast, as in West Coast, is what hip, groovy Americans like Hinton call California. I didn't know this at the time and got confused. I mean, New York is also on the coast.

much, but it's a bit scary here. It feels like this is the filter where all the mad people get stuck. People get shot for bumping into another car at the traffic-lights.'

'Listen, Robert. We don't all have guns, I've never had one. It's not that crazy here.' I tried to believe him, I tried to feel at home in this weird world. Hinton told me how he had lived in New York for twenty years and the worst thing that ever happened to him was being hit by a speeding bicycle.

'I'll tell you what, Hinton,' I said, having one of my ideas. 'I've always wanted to drive right across America. How about, if the series goes ahead, I meet you in New York, we buy some heap-of-shit big old car, and we drive across together?'

'Whoa!' said Hinton, laughing deeply in that special way only black men can. 'OK, like, I know I said not everyone is crazy and carries a gun, but I meant, like, in New York and LA. If you and I drove into some towns in the Midwest, we'd be in deep shit. If I was driving the police would think I had kidnapped you, so they'd shoot me. If the police didn't shoot me, some honky redneck would shoot you for being a nigger lover. If we come back here, baby, we fly!'

On the Friday night of the first week, all the men from the cast went out for a meal together at a branch of the California Pizza Kitchen. We had de-signer pizzas all round. I had a smoked chicken, pine-kernel-and-spinach pizza with Gruyère cheese and ham, sun-dried tomatoes, sliced dill cucumbers and mayonnaise on top. I think that's what it was. It didn't really look like a pizza: it looked like something you'd make for yourself late at night when you were stoned and had an attack of the munchies. Within five minutes of meeting these men I knew all about them, who they lived with, who they loved, who they hoped to love. They were incredibly open about their private lives, incredibly quickly.

On Saturday morning I stood in the foyer of the hotel with Andrea and her boyfriend Mickey. I had hired a car and we were going out shopping. That's what a lot of Californians do in their leisure time. They have stickers like BORN TO SHOP on the backs of their cars.

We had originally expected to go with Rob and Doug, who were desperate to go out and see Los Angeles, having never been there before. They had either been asleep in the hotel or on the set since the day we arrived. I knew they were not happy with the production, but I wasn't sure how unhappy. Rob and Doug were locked up in the big black tower* for the weekend, working with what sounded like three hundred comedy scriptwriters on the scripts. That sounds close enough to hell for me.

We visited a make-up superstore where Andrea was in heaven. Hundreds and thousands of jars of

---

* The big black tower is the headquarters building of Universal Television. It stands at one corner of the studio lot, and is big and black.

weird make-up, prosthetic remover, wigs, glue, false beards, all kinds of fake blood and eyeballs. We met a man there who'd made the masks for Warren Beatty's film *Dick Tracy*. The workshop at the back of the store had an extraordinary collection of rubber bits and pieces used in films, and we discovered that the place supplied the foam that made Kryten's head.

By the second week of rehearsals it was clear that a lot of shit had hit a lot of fans while I'd been rumbling around in my monster jeep. Rob and Doug had been banned from the set for overstepping the mark. They were present as advisers to the producers, but they were naturally worried that the show was going to get screwed up. I assumed they had tried to influence things too much and had trodden on some frayed egos.

The script had changed dramatically, and not, I have to say, that much for the better. We spent another day eating doughnuts and Danish, drinking coffee and wandering through the scenes in a half-hearted sort of way. We had a long break at one point, and I found out later that this was because Rob and Doug were having words with Linwood. I don't know what those words were exactly, but I don't think they were the sort you'd go to a church to hear.

Early the next morning a script was slipped under the door of my hotel room. I opened it, read it quickly and started laughing. It was funny and I knew why. The comedy boot boys had got tooled up and were cruising the mean streets looking for trouble. They were attempting a coup, spreading propaganda amongst the masses. It was thrilling. I met up with Hinton in the foyer.

'This is good shit,' he said, waving his copy of the script. 'Who did this?'

'The comedy police,' I said. 'Let's go watch the shit come down.'

As soon as we got to the studio it was clear everyone else had received a script too. The mood was much better.

'I like this one,' said Craig Bierko, holding the script aloft. 'This one is funny!'

The cast were asked to vote, can you believe it, on which script we preferred. It was a landslide for Rob and Doug: the comedy police had won the day. We all started to try and learn our lines for the first time. We'd been piddling about for ten days, then suddenly, with a virtually completely new script, we had only two days' rehearsal left. We were working hard suddenly, which was a bit of a shock but the show came together remarkably quickly. I really enjoyed working with the cast and felt more and more happy about doing a series with them, even if I secretly hoped it would be for only one year.

During the second day of rehearsal on the new script Elvin came up to me and said very loudly, 'Robert Llewellyn, phone call.' I found the phone hanging on a wall in a dark corner of the cavernous studio.

'Hello?'

'Hi, darl, it's me, in Ethiopia. You're not going to have plastic surgery are you?'

'Sorry?'

'You're not going to have a face-lift and have muscle implants in your legs are you?'

'I don't think so, darl,' I said. 'Why are you worried about it?'

Judy explained that a famous American actress had just flown in from Los Angeles and she looked a lot younger than she did in a TV series she'd made twenty years ago. Judy was worried that if we lived in Hollywood I'd get all sucked in by this and have face-lifts and hair transplants. I tried to assure her I wouldn't, that the people I was working with were really natural and I was bonding with them. This worried her more. She didn't think I'd ever bonded with anyone before. She was convinced I'd been sucked into Hollywood. She asked me if I'd been jogging. I said I hadn't, but I was thinking about going. This really upset her and she started crying. Elvin called me from across the studio. 'Robert Llewellyn, on set please.'

It's very difficult to be supportive to your partner at a time like that. I couldn't imagine where she was, so far away and in such a strange place. Judy knew LA better than I did: she'd worked there a lot in the past as a circus performer and acrobat. I had never been to Africa, let alone Ethiopia, so my mind was a blank when I tried to imagine what she was going through.

I said goodbye and rejoined the cast. I told them about my disturbing phone call and was showered with sympathy and support. I've never been accepted into such warm, embracing, bonding love so quickly anywhere on earth before. English actors can be a bit gushy or luvvie as I've said, but we don't have a patch on the Yanks. The women were virtually weeping as I told them how much I missed Judy. The men embraced me, telling me that knowing me, especially in my troubled time, was really important to them.

I was touched, I was bonding, but mainly with the men. I didn't do any of the bonding with women that can get you into trouble with your long-term, live-in, regular partner. The women in the cast were great, I really liked them, as sisters you understand. Lorraine, who played Captain Tao, was a lovely woman. Elizabeth Morehead, who played Kochanski, was a gorgeous woman. We all sat around and compared notes, who did we live with, when did we last have sex, what was it like. Michael Heintzman, who played Officer Munson, could vaguely remember having sex in the seventies, but he didn't think it was up to much. By this time in the rehearsals we all seemed to know everything about each other. This is the up-side to luvviedom. I never felt lonely in Los Angeles and I know from previous experience it can be a very lonely town.

Just to balance out the whole California-is-full-of-natural-people-who-relate-to-each-other-on-a-meaningful-level notion, I need to relate the story of the Zeppelin invasion. The twenty-five women who came into the studio on the day before the pre-record were unbelievable.

In the American pilot, there was a sequence where Lister showed Kryten a hologramatic device which hides the fact that his bed is a mess and contains an illicit cat.* The hologramatic images shown were his bed all neat and tidy like Rimmer's and another where a semi-naked, beautiful blonde woman lay in a languorous pose on his bed.

We arrived for rehearsal to find the studio crawling with women who had what seemed to be large, tightly stuffed pieces of Ikea furniture attached to their chests. I was completely dumbstruck. All the women auditioning for this part had undergone breast-implant surgery of mind-boggling proportions. They wore super-skin-tight bright yellow T-shirts, but they didn't look real. They looked like Barbie dolls. They all had big hair, which is a thing English women don't have. American women seem to be able to grow their hair bigger, huge piles of fluff which are real but don't look it. Interestingly enough, the woman who finally got the gig of lying on Lister's bed and having her picture taken was the only one present who didn't look like she had implants.

Suddenly on the pre-record day it was like work again. I was up at the crack of dawn, moaning and

* The cat of whom the Cat is an ancestor.

complaining with Andrea. It was like the good old days. On went the mask, and the new Kryten smiled right across his big square head. It was so comfortable: no rubber around my mouth or nostrils and no glue close to my eyes. The man who made the American mask is a god of prosthetics, a living legend of mechano-human comfort. With the mask on, and after receiving suitable fantastics and ooohs and that is incredibles from the director and cast, I headed for the costume department.

The men who had covered me in plaster bandage and measured my every organ had come up trumps. A Kryten costume of splendid comfort, durability, flexibility and damn fine looks. I could sit in it, walk in it, turn in it, I could almost look sexy in it.* I was a happy robot as I stomped on to the set. I marched up to Rob and Doug. I wanted them to see what I had been on about all those years. This was just how I always wanted Kryten to be. 'Guys,' I said, 'what d'you think?'

Doug started to walk around me, staring at the wonderful detail and splendid cut of my chest piece, the snug fit of the Lycra body suit, the gentle curves of the neck ribbing.

'Yeah, no, yeah, no, it's yeah, no,' said Doug, nodding and raising his eyebrows.

'It looks pony, Bobby,' said Rob after a while. I

---

* I still couldn't pee in it. I had to be unbolted, un-Velcroed and unpeeled to get out of the damn thing.

was heartbroken. Pony was the worst Rob Grant criticism. If something looked pony, that was it.

'I think it looks great,' I said in a pathetically defensive way.

'No, the costume's OK, the mask looks pony,' said Rob. 'It's pony, Bobby.'

'Yeah, no, yeah. Pony,' said Doug.

'Pony, Bobby,' said Rob.

'Is it comfortable though?' asked Doug.

'It's never going to be comfortable,' I whined, 'but it's bloody amazing in comparison with the old one.'

'You look greaeaeaeaeat,' said Linwood, joining us.

'Pony,' said Rob, lighting a cigarette. I knew the bone of contention between us would continue.*

There were about three hundred more members of the crew than there were in England. They earn more money, they drive bigger cars, they eat more, they laugh more, their bottoms are considerably larger but other than that they are very similar. The director was calm and reassuring, Linwood was happy and loving and well bonded and secure. Rob and Doug, who were back on the set in a big way, were looking the same as ever. Dishevelled, shagged out and totally focused on the job.

As the cast gathered to make an entrance before a scene, I was assing about doing silly walks and voices

---

* I have to say, now that I have seen the mask on the screen, the English one looks better. Damn. The American one looks like a bloke with rubber stuck to his head. There's no way round it.

as I normally do. In a similar situation in the English series, Craig Charles would quite likely be trying to set fire to the set with his Zippo lighter just before we go on. Chris might be telling me about his straight-eight 3.5L E-type engine, introduced in the early sixties. Danny might be showing us some dance steps from the musical *Les Misérables*, or doing a drag run and laughing very loudly. Someone shouts action and we go on.

Not so with the American cast. As I did a comedy walk up the corridor and tried to copulate with part of the set, Craig and Chris asked me if I wouldn't mind stopping. 'I'm sorry, Robert, but I really have to focus a moment here,' said Chris. 'Would you please stop fucking the sliding door?'

'Sorry, sorry,' I said. I felt awful. I would hate to be thrown by another actor in a situation like that. I was so used to the atmosphere in the old *Red Dwarf*, I had completely lost my manners.

We finished at something like six in the evening. Andrea cleaned off the mask and I showered in my dressing room, receiving the standard amount of static electric shocks. Los Angeles is basically built on a desert, and I suppose it's something to do with the air and the temperature and the nylon carpet, but everything I touched sent such a bolt of static through me my hair stood on end.

I met up with Hinton and we went to the movies in my big rumbling jeep. I admit now that I saw *Freejack*, a movie with Mick Jagger in it. It is quite an embarrassing thing to have to admit that you paid money to go and see a film like *Freejack*. Mick Jagger, what an actor! That's all I can say.

The following day Elvin Ivory turned up driving his Thursday Porsche, a green one. He has one for each day of the week, each of them especially adapted to take his amazing six-foot-ten-inch frame.

'Good morning, Robert Llewellyn,' he said with a big grin as he strode past me. We had a script meeting, yet more changes but none very major, and then we camera blocked the show which was going to be recorded in front of the audience.

They recorded two versions of the show that day, one in the afternoon without an audience, one in the evening with. I had to put my make-up on during the lunch break ready for the full recorded dress run in the afternoon.

In the evening I entered the studio with the rest of the cast and we hid behind the set. The atmosphere was transformed. There was an audience of about five hundred, most of whom had seen the British series. We were introduced one by one, and I have to say, and it's not often this happens, and I'm normally humble, and I've never hungered for stardom, but I have to say they went apeshit when I walked on to the set. I have never received such a welcome from an audience, it was incredible.

I can safely say that evening was one of the top two or three *Red Dwarf* recordings I have been involved in from an audience response point of view.

They absolutely loved it; they laughed at everything and they roared laughing at Kryten. I have never enjoyed making an episode of *Red Dwarf* more. I wasn't hot, I wasn't too uncomfortable, and I had loads of gags and no big speeches explaining triplicators and time dilation.

At the end the men in suits from NBC Television, the broadcasters who were due to buy the show and the men in suits from Universal who were due to make the show, all came up to meet me. I have never shaken so many hands in one evening, in costume. People queued up to have their picture taken with me. I stood next to a very rich man in a suit and pulled a face into a camera. He shook my hand and said, 'You are going to be a major star here, Robert. Fantastic performance.'

I thanked him and saw Rob and Doug looking at me. 'Bobby,' said Rob as he hugged me, 'well done, we've done it, man, it's fantastic.'

Doug gave me a big hug, 'Yeah, yeah, great, yeah,' he said. 'Hey, are you the popular one tonight or what?'

Elvin Ivory walked up to me and embraced me, my head came up to his tummy button. 'Robert Llewellyn, you were great, that was a really funny performance. Listen, the boss of NBC was in tonight, he loved it. I'm telling you, I've been in this business a long time. I'm telling you, this show is going to run, and you, Robert Llewellyn, are going to be a . . .'

I thanked him, I thanked everyone, I was well brought up. Andrea came up to me and told me I had been clear for ten minutes and how come I hadn't run screaming into my dressing room. She couldn't believe what was going on. The whole studio was full of people embracing each other, patting each other on the back. Elvin was passing around peak caps with I RODE THE RED DWARF embossed on the front. Champagne bottles popped open, and Linwood gave me a plastic cup full: 'Robert, what can I say? You were really amazing. I can't tell you how proud I am to have worked with you. This show is going to run, I can feel it, man. And you were so good, so funny, you've worked so hard. It's incredible, man, did you hear that audience? They loved it, man. Hey, are you pleased I talked you into it?'

I told him I was very pleased. I drank my champagne and hugged the cast. We all kept hugging and kissing and drinking champagne for what seemed like ages. I eventually stumbled somewhat groggily back to my dressing room with Andrea. As she peeled the mask off, there was a constant flow of people coming into the room: the cast, the director, Rob and Doug, Linwood. I was sitting in my Calvin Klein briefs with a rubber head on looking like ET. No one minded. It was party time.

We all retired to the lobby of the hotel, waiters brought more and more champagne, Linwood and Rob and Doug seemed to have made up. Jeff Field was inviting me over to his house to ride his polo ponies. He came to England regularly to play polo, sometimes with Prince Charles.

Getting to bed took me ages, there were so many people to say goodbye to, so many people to promise to keep in touch with. I collapsed with exhaustion at about three in the morning and crawled to bed, not before we had all swapped numbers and addresses. Rob and Doug had to get up at eight and fly back to London to complete series five in England.

I was woken at nine the following morning by my phone.

'Hi, Robert, this is Harvey Greenstein. I saw you last night in *Red Dwarf*. You were fantastic, I'm just ringing, really informally, to see if you have representation here.'

He was an agent, he was after my ass.

'I've got an agent in London,' I said, trying to speak through the dead vermin on my tongue. Being a very light drinker, I only have to sniff alcohol and I have the mother of hangovers the following morning.

'Sure, but you need someone to look out for you over here. Why don't we meet up for lunch and talk it over, in a completely informal way? Let's go to Musso and Frank's.'

No sooner had I scribbled down some information about when and where I'd meet this guy than the phone rang again.

'Hi, Robert, I was given your number by Mona, my name's Richard Williams, I saw you last night in *Red Dwarf* and I thought you were . . .'

After the third call I asked reception to take messages and let me sleep. But was no good: my mind was racing with what was happening to me. As I was in the shower I realized that I was potentially very hot property for an agent. I was an actor out on a limb with a ready-made income. They didn't have to do anything except increase my income, rake off their ten per cent and go out to lunch with me occasionally.

At reception there were eight messages and five faxes waiting for me. I felt like a very important person all of a sudden. I needed to spend some time on my own to remind myself that I wasn't important at all. I am old enough to remember that I only feel important and special if people tell me I am. As soon as I'm alone I remember the truth.

I threw my small bag into the vast cavern of my rumbling jeep and drove down the road ten miles or so to my favourite diner. It was crowded and busy and no one recognized me or told me I was great. I had a huge gut-busting breakfast with ten cups of coffee. I read all my faxes and messages, many of which were from London, where my book *The Reconstructed Heart* was receiving a lot of attention. I had to get back there to promote it. I had written articles for the *Guardian*, *The Times* and the *Daily Mail*. I filled in a questionnaire from *City Limits* magazine and sat back to think. However much I tried to remember that I wasn't important and things were really just normal, I was being swept along with the thought that I was going to be rich and famous and live in America.

I handed the parking attendant my ticket outside the diner, he delivered my huge rumbler to the kerb, and I drove over the hill into Hollywood. I had a lunch appointment at Musso and Frank's, an old-fashioned restaurant on Hollywood Boulevard. I was meeting Harvey Greenstein, the agent who had woken me up.

'Robert,' said Harvey, 'it's great to meet you.' We moved to a small cubicle at the back of the restaurant.

'Whaddaya want?' said a very old, tight-skinned waiter. I'm not sure if the waiters at Musso and Frank's have a reputation for being very rude, but if they don't, I'm starting one. They are also very funny.

'We'll have water, and a menu already,' said Harvey Greenstein, not fazed at all. He turned back to me eagerly. 'This is great, Robert, you are such a talented actor, you're a star in England, right?'

'Well, no, to be honest I don't think I could claim that.'

'Stop being so modest already. If you're not, it's their loss, because you are going to be massive here, the white Eddie Murphy, you are so funny, with your walks and your voices. Listen,' he said conspiratorially, 'you will make so much money here with that kind of talent.'

'Well, I don't know, I mean it was only a pilot.'

'But what a pilot! It'll run, believe me. Tell me, what are you making on the show?'

I wasn't sure what to say. I still felt the natural British reticence when it came to talking about money. He started throwing around ballpark figures, and I eventually nodded when he came down as low as mine.

'Oy, what are you doing, charity work?' he said happily. 'You know what Ted Danson gets?' I told him I knew it was a million an episode. 'That's for one transmission. He gets eighty per cent for a repeat. Robert, I can guarantee that for the first year I will get you between fifty and seventy-five thousand dollars an ep. OK, so this year that's six eps in a mid-season replacement, so you're looking at three hundred to four and a half hundred thousand dollars. That's just to start, then, next year, thirty-six episodes, we go in gentle, a hundred thou an ep, rising to a hundred fifty in summer. Now you're looking at about three and a half million a year.' He paused and stared into my eyes, presumably looking for signs of delight. He could sense my misgivings. 'Pre-tax of course, I'm talking gross, but even after every deduction there is, you're walking away with two million bucks in your pocket. It's big money, Robert, and you just fell right in it. How did you do it? I'll tell you, with talent, that's what sells in this town.'

After lunch I left Harvey on the pavement, waving at me furiously as I gunned my rumbler back over the hill. I was staying with Jane Leeves in her apartment in Studio City. Her apartment has a spare room: we did not do anything kinky. I fell asleep and didn't wake up until the following day.

I went with Jane to see her agent, who also told me I was the greatest thing since sliced bread. He worked in a big black tower on Sunset Boulevard in a company called CAA, a huge agency which looks after thousands of actors.

'So you want to live in LA?' he said cheerfully.

'Um, not really,' I said, 'but if I have to I will.'

'You have to, Robert, because that show is going to run.'

'Right,' I said.

'If you ever want to talk about representation, you know where I am, give me a call. I guess you've been chased a bit, huh?' I nodded. 'Don't worry about it, you'll do good. You are hot property now, Robert. This always happens when there's a new talent in town. This town is talent hungry, and you've got buckets to sell.'

On the way out to a restaurant that evening, Jane told me her agent never bullshitted, he was a straight-down-the-line guy. But I was getting more and more calls from London, and it was clear I had to get back. The following day I caught a plane to New York, first class American Airlines, all paid for by the way. If I'd been paying, I would have flown super-bucket-shop economy, bring your own packed lunch. The food wasn't quite as good as Qantas, but there was plenty of it, and masses of room.

New York was snowbound and bitterly cold. I stayed with old friends for two nights in up-state New York, spent a day with Chris Eigman in Manhattan, saw Boris Yeltsin arrive by helicopter at the Battery, by chance that is, I hadn't arranged it with Boris, and had a great meal at La Indochine restaurant with Chris. This is the place where drop-dead beautiful people queue to get a job as wait-persons because they are supposed to get spotted for movie parts. They were all drop-dead beautiful, but I didn't think any of them were going to get a gig, to be honest.

I flew back to London first class. It was so luxurious and proper, so rich feeling and special making. I got on the tube at Heathrow and headed for my small flat in Islington. Suddenly the specialness and richness and glamour started to feel like old party clothes. I was back to normal, back to London, my pushbike, the rain, the homeless people, the telephone bills, the dust, the shopping that needed doing. Judy was still in Ethiopia and there was no one at my flat. It was warm, but hollow. There was a big pile of mail for me. None of the letters was from Hollywood. There was no contract, there was no demand for me to get on the next flight out there and start shooting the series.

Likewise my answer machine. There were many messages, but none from Universal Television, none from some agent saying, 'Bob, they want you to take Mel Gibson's part in *Lethal Weapon 3*.' Nothing. I made a cup of tea and sat in silence, back to normal.

It was all right really. I wasn't sad, I was just waiting to calm down again.

The irony light in the giant control room in the sky had been going on my section for a long time. However, every now and then, when there is some heavy irony going down somewhere on earth, you get a break. There was no irony going through my mainframe as I sat in my kitchen. I was in an irony-free zone. It was only a temporary glitch, but while it lasted, it was very, very peaceful.

Discover more about our forthcoming books through Penguin's FREE newspaper...

Penguin
Quarterly

It's packed with:

- exciting features
- author interviews
- previews & reviews
- books from your favourite films & TV series
- exclusive competitions & much, much more...

Write off for your free copy today to:
Dept JC
Penguin Books Ltd
FREEPOST
West Drayton
Middlesex
UB7 0BR
NO STAMP REQUIRED

READ MORE IN PENGUIN

In every corner of the world, on every subject under the sun, Penguin represents quality and variety – the very best in publishing today.

For complete information about books available from Penguin – including Puffins, Penguin Classics and Arkana – and how to order them, write to us at the appropriate address below. Please note that for copyright reasons the selection of books varies from country to country.

In the United Kingdom: Please write to *Dept. JC, Penguin Books Ltd, FREEPOST, West Drayton, Middlesex UB7 0BR*

If you have any difficulty in obtaining a title, please send your order with the correct money, plus ten per cent for postage and packaging, to *PO Box No. 11, West Drayton, Middlesex UB7 0BR*

In the United States: Please write to *Penguin USA Inc., 375 Hudson Street, New York, NY 10014*

In Canada: Please write to *Penguin Books Canada Ltd, 10 Alcorn Avenue, Suite 300, Toronto, Ontario M4V 3B2*

In Australia: Please write to *Penguin Books Australia Ltd, 487 Maroondah Highway, Ringwood, Victoria 3134*

In New Zealand: Please write to *Penguin Books (NZ) Ltd, 182–190 Wairau Road, Private Bag, Takapuna, Auckland 9*

In India: Please write to *Penguin Books India Pvt Ltd, 706 Eros Apartments, 56 Nehru Place, New Delhi 110 019*

In the Netherlands: Please write to *Penguin Books Netherlands B.V., Keizersgracht 231 NL–1016 DV Amsterdam*

In Germany: Please write to *Penguin Books Deutschland GmbH, Friedrichstrasse 10–12, W–6000 Frankfurt/Main 1*

In Spain: Please write to *Penguin Books S. A., C. San Bernardo 117–6º E–28015 Madrid*

In Italy: Please write to *Penguin Italia s.r.l., Via Felice Casati 20, I–20124 Milano*

In France: Please write to *Penguin France S. A., 17 rue Lejeune, F–31000 Toulouse*

In Japan: Please write to *Penguin Books Japan, Ishikiribashi Building, 2–5–4, Suido, Bunkyo-ku, Tokyo 112*

In Greece: Please write to *Penguin Hellas Ltd, Dimocritou 3, GR–106 71 Athens*

In South Africa: Please write to *Longman Penguin Southern Africa (Pty) Ltd, Private Bag X08, Bertsham 2013*

Red Dwarf Grant Naylor

When Lister got drunk, he got really drunk.

After celebrating his birthday with a Monopoly-board pub crawl around London, he came to in a burger bar on one of Saturn's moons, wearing a lady's pink crimplene hat and a pair of yellow fishing waders, with no money and a passport in the name of Emily Berkenstein.

Joining the Space Corps seemed a good idea. *Red Dwarf*, a clapped-out spaceship, was bound for Earth. It never made it, leaving Lister as the last remaining member of the human race, three million years from Earth, with only a dead man, a senile computer and a highly evolved cat for company.

They begin their journey home. On the way they'll break the Light Barrier. They'll meet Einstein, Archimedes, God and Norman Wisdom ... and discover an alternative plane of Reality.

READ MORE IN PENGUIN

Better Than Life   Grant Naylor

Lister is lost. Three million years from Earth he's marooned in a world created by his own psyche. For Lister it's the most dangerous place he could possibly be because he's completely happy.

Rimmer has a problem too. He's dead. But that's not the problem. Rimmer's problem is that he's trapped in a landscape controlled by his own subconscious. And Rimmer's subconscious doesn't like him one little bit.

Together with Cat, the best-dressed entity in all six known universes, and Kryten, a sanitation Mechanoid with a missing sanity chip, they are trapped in the ultimate computer game: Better Than Life. The zenith of computer-game technology, BTL transports you directly to a perfect world of your imagination, a world where you can enjoy fabulous wealth and unmitigated success.

It's the ideal game with only one drawback – it's so good, it will kill you.

and:

The Red Dwarf Omnibus

READ MORE IN PENGUIN

Primordial Soup   Grant Naylor

Before recorded Time, there existed a substance known as Primordial Soup. From this disgustingly unpromising, gunky substance, all life began. Likewise, from the disgustingly unpromising, gunky scripts, sprang the disgusting, gunky comedy series, *Red Dwarf*.

Primordial Soup is a selection of the least worst scripts from the first five years of *Red Dwarf*, tracing the series from its humble beginnings to its humble present.

Each of the scripts has been personally chosen by the author from his rubber-sheeted bed in the Norfolk Nursing Home for the Intellectually Challenged.

The Making of Red Dwarf   Joe Nazzaro

Behind the scenes in deep space Shepperton, American journalist Joe Nazzaro spent three months with the *Red Dwarf* cast and crew during the shooting of Series VI.

This is a fascinating account of how an ambitious and technically complex TV show is translated from script to screen, together with interviews and observations from the stars, writers, producers and production team.

How close are the stars to their real characters?

Where do the ideas for the series come from?

Are the multi-award-winning model sequences really shot in outer space?

Packed with stunning behind-the-scenes photographs, with an introduction by the series' creators Rob Grant and Doug Naylor, this book is not only an unmissable treat for *Red Dwarf* fans, but a valuable reference work on how a television series is made.

READ MORE IN PENGUIN

HUMOUR

The Quest for the Big Woof   Lenny Henry and Steve Parkhouse

What is the Big Woof? Perplexed by the question, and with a deadline to meet, Lenny Henry sets off to find the philosopher's stone that turns pain into laughter.

Be a Bloody Train Driver   Jacky Fleming

Jacky Fleming takes a wry, original look at women's (and girls') lives in these brilliantly funny cartoons.

Alex V: The Man with the Golden Handshake
Charles Peattie and Russell Taylor

Alex, hero of the *Independent*'s business pages, faces the ultimate indignity: not only has he been made redundant, but people seem to think he has hired his dinner jacket for the charity ball. Meanwhile, Greg, Alex's journalist brother, is roughing it in the desert reporting on the Gulf War ... and claiming expenses for the Riyadh Hilton.

How to Become Ridiculously Well-read in One Evening
E. O. Parrot

Contains some 150 succinct and entertaining encapsulations of the best-known books in the English language, including a few foreign works familiar to us in translation. 'Very funny. Well calculated to put all teachers of English Literature in their places' – John Mortimer

READ MORE IN PENGUIN

A SELECTION OF FICTION AND NON-FICTION

Brightside G. H. Morris

Stuffed with magic, coal grit and wayward, Rabelaisian humour, this wonderful trilogy chronicles the lives of three generations of the Brightsides – a family with an appetite for the extraordinary. 'We've just mined a seam of home-produced – and Northern – magic realism' – *Observer*

Chasing the Monsoon Alexander Frater

In 1987 Alexander Frater decided to pursue the astonishing phenomenon of the Indian summer monsoon and this fascinating account of his journey reveals the exotic, often startling discoveries of an ambitious and irresistibly romantic adventure.

Love in the Time of Cholera Gabriel García Márquez

'For fifty years a breath-taking beauty, now old and just widowed, has recoiled in pride and guilt from her secret lover. His desolate obsession has led him into an enigmatic existence in spite of his renown in business. One Pentecost, love found a new tongue with which to speak. Unique Márquez magic of the sadness and funniness of humanity' – *The Times*

The Invisible Woman Claire Tomalin

'Made visible is Nelly Ternan, and in the process, Tomalin gives us the world of a nineteenth-century actress and most importantly, the real world of Charles Dickens, whose passion for her ... changed his life, his career and his work' – Melvyn Bragg in the *Independent*

Shots from the Hip Charles Shaar Murray

His classic encapsulation of the moment when rock stars turned junkies as the sixties died; his dissection of rock 'n' roll violence as citizens assaulted the Sex Pistols; his superstar encounters, from the decline of Paul McCartney to Mick Jagger's request that the author should leave – Charles Shaar Murray's *Shots from the Hip* is also rock history in the making.

READ MORE IN PENGUIN

A SELECTION OF FICTION AND NON-FICTION

Money for Nothing   P. G. Wodehouse

Lester Carmody of Rudge Hall is not altogether a good egg. Rather the reverse, in fact. For his intention is to inherit a large sum from the family silver by arranging its theft… 'His whimsical, hilarious stories aimed to do nothing more than amuse' – *Sunday Express*

Lucky Jim   Kingsley Amis

'Dixon makes little dents in the smug fabric of hypocritical, humbugging, classbound British society … Amis caught the mood of post-war restiveness in a book which, though socially significant, was, and still is, extremely funny' – Anthony Burgess

The Day Gone By   Richard Adams

'He is the best adventure-story-writer alive … Answers to the literary and personal puzzles of the Mr Adams phenomenon lie buried like truffles in his admirable autobiography' – A. N. Wilson in the *Daily Telegraph*

Romancing Vietnam   Justin Wintle

'Justin Wintle's journal is a memorable, often amusing, always interesting diary of a tour of duty in a land where sharp-end history pokes round every corner' – *Yorkshire Post*. 'Compelling reading' – *Sunday Telegraph*

Travelling the World   Paul Theroux

Now, for the first time, Paul Theroux has authorized a book of his favourite travel writing, containing photographs taken by those who have followed in his footsteps. The exquisite pictures here brilliantly complement and illuminate the provocative, wry, witty commentaries of one of the world's greatest travellers.

READ MORE IN PENGUIN

A SELECTION OF FICTION AND NON-FICTION

A Start in Life Anita Brookner

Now forty, Dr Ruth Weiss looks back and tells the story of a life impassioned and seduced by literature. As she recalls her London childhood, her friendships and doomed Parisian love affairs, she knows that once again she must make a start in life.

The Shape of Love Gelsey Kirkland and Greg Lawrence

In this compelling sequel to her bestselling *Dancing on My Grave,* Gelsey Kirkland takes up the story as she returns to the London stage to star as Juliet in *Romeo and Juliet* and Princess Aurora in *Sleeping Beauty.* 'Heart-rending ... the very image of passion' – *Observer*

The Life and Death of Mary Wollstonecraft Claire Tomalin

'Wide, penetrating, sympathetic ... there is no better book on Mary Wollstonecraft, nor is there likely to be ... The author brings a deep understanding to a remarkably complex woman ... but it is more than a biography: it illuminates the radical world of the 1780s and 1790s as few others do' – *New Statesman*

Isabelle Annette Kobak
The Life of Isabelle Eberhardt

'A European turned Arab, a Christian turned Muslim, a woman dressed as a man; a libertine who stilled profound mystical cravings by drink, hashish and innumerable Arab lovers ... All the intricate threads of her rebellious life are to be found in Annette Kobak's scrupulously researched book' – *Daily Telegraph*

Going Too Far Caroline Lassalle

On the terrace of a Greek villa Bettina and her guests – malicious, unstable Johnny and dedicated but excessive Delia – pass the morning, afternoon and evening of one day in quarrels, reminiscences and the telling of classical myths and legends. 'A brilliant and emotionally satisfying book' – *Sunday Times*